Endorsement

At Maxwell Leadership, we believe that leadership is about making a difference through values-based influence. That's why we are honored to partner with William Brunson—a leader who exemplifies service and creating lasting impact. As a Maxwell Leadership Certified Team member, William is committed to living out our mission: to equip and empower others to lead with integrity, purpose, and passion. We're in the business of adding value to people, and William is a shining example of that mission in action.

—**Chris Robinson,** *EVP, Maxwell Leadership*

Faith, Leadership, and Walt

*Leading with Purpose, Passion,
and the Power of Possibility*

Dr. William B. Brunson

PB ISBN: 979-8-9943813-8-0
E-book ISBN: 979-8-9943813-9-7

Dedication

To Michelle,

My beautiful wife—the person with whom I get to experience life, ministry, and every dream worth pursuing. Your love, faith, and unwavering support make all things possible.

Contents

Opening Thoughts

For the leaders who wake up every morning and lead with their heart rooted in passion, compassion, and unwavering conviction, I share this with you. May these pages be a mirror, reflecting to you the God-given potential within and a window into what your leadership can enable in the lives of others when it's exercised with courage, compassion, and purpose.

This is a book for the dreamers and doers; those who are willing to strive; those who believe in serving a God whose power is not only in the past but is in the present too; those who know that vision and persistence and resilience are the tools that God often uses to change hearts... and by changing hearts, changes history.

This book is for people of faith—for Christians who want to grow as disciples and to lead lives of purpose and significance. You may not call yourself a Christian leader—either at work, at home, or anywhere else that life takes you—but you are. John Maxwell has said, "Leadership is influence—nothing more and nothing less." As a Christian, you are called to lead because you are called to influence the world for Christ. Ever since the Great Commission was given (that we should be disciples who make disciples) the expectation has been that we will lead and influence—our home, our school, our work, our play—for Christ.

Anywhere and everywhere—as a follower of Christ, you are a leader for Christ.

I am writing this book for you at a point in my life where I have nearly thirty-five years of experience in leading and learning to lead. I've had moments when I was hitting on all cylinders and helping others grow in their skills and influence. I've also had seasons where I was so lost I was actually in the way of just about everyone else. If you have ever been in either of those places (and I know you have), this is the book for you.

One of the greatest creative leaders and innovators in history was Walt Disney. I know that according to many of you, he's the "cartoon guy," but he invented genres, transformed an industry, and developed technology the world had never seen. While neither I nor this book have any association with Disney (though I visit their theme parks as often as I can), this book is based on countless years of self-exploration and digging into the fascinating stories of Walt.

Walt Disney's legacy is an astonishing testament that dreams, approached with imagination and perseverance, can lead to outright transformation. My hope is that this book will encourage you to receive and walk in the calling God has for you. Whatever you are building from castles to schools, businesses to ministries, the guidance of your faith does matter.

As I write this book, I am also reflecting on the faith that has made me and has shaped my life. You see, at nineteen years old, I responded to the call of ministry, and ever since that day I have been pastoring churches. On my first Sunday as a pastor, I preached to a congregation of one person (That added a bit of pressure to the offering/donation part in the service.). I'm now pastoring a church of more than 3,400 souls. So much has changed over the years, but Scripture is still Scripture, faith is still faith, leadership is still leadership.

So, for a Christian (at home, at work, at school, at church), it is faith that is the stable and solid ground upon which we can build our leadership. As you continue to read, just remember: Leadership is something that can be taught and cultivated; role models (such as Walt) and mentors are important, personal courage in leadership and spiritual growth (for both leaders and followers) are possible. With God—there is no mountain that is too high or dream too impossible to reach.

Read, Learn, Grow!
Bill

PS: As you read, I will be going back and forth between many biblical people who make up our faith story and the stories from Walt Disney's life. The answer to the question you might be asking is: No, I don't equate Walt with anyone in the Bible. I have benefited from the lesson of successes and failures that I have found in his life, and I wanted to share some of them with you.

Walt, Leadership, and Faith

Walt Disney wasn't setting out to give us a handbook for Christian leadership in how he ran his businesses. However, in his values of staying vision focused and seeking excellence while also being a servant leader, and doing it with integrity—we find Biblical values lived out. His example demonstrates the effectiveness of God's pattern of leadership, since it reflects how the Lord designed organizations and relationships to operate at their best.

Faith was an integral part of Walt's life. He was raised in a home that instilled Christian virtues and values into his life. Walt Disney was named after Reverend Walter Parr, who preached at St. Paul Congregational Church in Chicago that the Disney family attended when he was born. Walt was baptized in that church on June 8, 1902.

When the family moved to Marceline, Missouri, they immediately joined the Congregational Church near their home. In an article in 1949, Walt said, "I believe firmly in the efficacy of religion, in its powerful influence on a person's whole life. It helps immeasurably to meet the storm and stress of life and keep you attuned to the Divine inspiration. Without inspiration, we would perish."

At other times, when Walt spoke about his faith, he said,

"All I ask of myself is to live a good Christian life and toward that objective I bend every effort in shaping my personal, domestic and professional activities and growth."

"Most things are good, and they are the strongest things; but there are evil things too, and you are not doing a child a favor by trying to shield them from reality. The important thing to teach a child is that good always triumphs over evil, and that is what our pictures attempt to do."

"Both my study of Scripture and my career in entertaining children have taught me to cherish them."

"I have a strong personal belief and reliance on the power of prayer for divine inspiration. Every person has his own ideas of the act of praying for God's guidance, tolerance and mercy to fulfill his duties and responsibilities."

"My own concept of prayer is not as a plea for special favors or as a quick palliation for wrongs knowingly committed. A prayer, it seems to me, implies a promise as well as a request."

"In these days of world tensions, when the faith of men is being tested as never before, I am personally thankful that my parents taught me at a very early age to have a strong personal belief and reliance in the power of prayer for Divine inspiration."

"Every person has his own ideas of the act of praying for God's guidance, tolerance, and mercy to fulfill his duties and responsibilities. My own concept of prayer is not as a plea for special favors nor as a quick palliation for wrongs knowingly committed. A prayer, it seems to me, implies a promise as well as a request; at the highest level, prayer not only is a supplication for strength and guidance, but also becomes an affirmation of life and thus a reverent praise of God."

"Deeds rather than words express my concept of the part religion should play in everyday life. I have watched constantly that in our movie work the highest moral and spiritual standards are upheld, whether it deals with fable or with stories of living action."

"Whatever success I have had in bringing clean, informative entertainment to people of all ages, I attribute in great part to my Congregational upbringing and my lifelong habit of prayer."

"To me, today, at age sixty-one, all prayer, by the humble or highly placed, has one thing in common: supplication for strength and inspiration to carry on the best human impulses which should bind us together for a better world."

Walt's belief that "deeds rather than words" was a driving factor of his life, and is a lesson that we may need to learn. Too often our words sound more faithful than our deeds demonstrate. While, like us, Walt never described himself as a Christian leader—his faith in God and deep belief in prayer were the guideposts of his life.

Our Advantage

As I said earlier, as Christians we are called to influence our world for Christ, which means we are all called to be leaders in His name. As Christian leaders we have a few things going for us:

We have the Scripture available to us -- which is full of straightforward leadership principles, character-forming truth, and organizational well-being. There's no necessity of handling life with trial and error alone, but instead we can glean from Biblical leaders and apply proven truth to our situations.

We are given the Holy Spirit, who provides us with wisdom for difficult decisions, strength for the hard seasons of life, and even love for difficult people. We don't have to lead in our own strength—we can tap into the endless strength and grace of God.

We belong to the Christian family, and through that connection we have accountability, encouragement, and fellowship in our victories as well as our struggles. We don't have to do the work of leadership alone—we can lean on the prayers, wisdom, and friendship of other believers.

We have the benefit of an eternal perspective, can act with kingdom purpose, and not just for short-term results here and now. We don't have to judge success only according to human standards; we can measure our leadership in terms of whether it serves God's purposes and moves forward some portion of his kingdom.

These advantages do not promise that Christian leadership will be easy, or that we won't experience failures or setbacks. As you'll see, Walt Disney's life illustrates that effective leadership always involves risk, personal sacrifice, and the need for perseverance in difficult seasons.

But as Christian leaders, we can lead with the confidence of knowing that our work has eternal significance, that God will provide what we need to accomplish His call on our lives and ministry, and that the faithful stewardship of our legacy will produce fruit that far outlives us.

INTRODUCTION

Why This Book Matters Now

We live in an age of shallow and loud leadership—leadership that is fast not farsighted. We need real Christian leaders, now more than ever—people of ability, people of character—visionaries who live and lead with biblical principles as their guide.

Yes, in this book, we will look at the leadership and legacy of Walt Disney. We will be seeing everything through the prism of one of history's most innovative minds: Walt himself. Yet at the same time, this book is a journey that is grounded in the eternal truths, which we find in Scripture. We are going to learn, step by step, how faith has a bearing on the leader's heart and motivation for action—the leader's vision and ultimate authority.

You'll also learn how the stories of biblical leaders—from Moses to Nehemiah, Esther to Paul—provide models that modern-day leaders can emulate. There is still life in these old stories; they resonate in boardrooms, classrooms, and at kitchen tables—truly, wherever influence is wielded today.

You will read how Walt Disney's revolutionary approach to quality, vision, and magic, all bring to light the importance of focusing on "ideals" and never settling for "less."

My prayer for you is that this book will enable you to lead with more clarity, courage, and conviction in your God-given circle of influence.

Here's my hope:

1. That you will think of the Kingdom in a culture of self.
2. That you will discover how biblical wisdom guides us to make visionary decisions.
3. That you will grow to use your words to convincingly convey your passion.
4. That the trials you encounter will make you stronger and never break your spirit.
5. That you will mature into a humble, truthful, and unwavering leader.

You may be leading a multi-billion-dollar company, leading a mission ministry, or simply leading your own family... this book was written to help you lead better.

So, here's the invitation: be brave. Lead with conviction and never cease building the future you want to see in your own lifetime.

If you lead people, you are changing eternity. Let's do it well.

CHAPTER ONE

The Vision That Changes Everything

Purpose and Vision

When his daughters were little, every Saturday was "Daddy's Day" for Walt Disney. That often required a trip to Griffith Park in Los Angeles, to watch his two young daughters giggle as they stretched for the brass rings on an old carousel. Walt would sit on the bench and wave at his daughters when they passed for a lap, watching as other parents did the same. For most people, that was it—just another Saturday in the park by the old carousel. Not Walt. He saw something else altogether. He wasn't focused on the chipped paint or listening to the mechanical groans of a creaky old carousel. Walt started dreaming of a place where families played together—a world where parents and children, whatever their age, could explore together and stay connected forever. He dreamed of a place where they could share the marvel of creativity—a place where imagination could run wild and dreams could take flight.

That vision would become Disneyland—the place that redefined entertainment even as it changed millions of lives forever. But here's what makes the story remarkable:

1

Walt didn't merely envision a theme park. He saw the future. Where others saw problems, he spotted opportunity. Where others saw limits, he saw potential.

Sound familiar? For people of faith—it's a narrative heard over and over again in Scripture. So many stories in the Bible challenge people to lift up their gaze beyond the here and now, to look at what can be, could be, should be. There is one such incident that dates back 4,000+ years. Another man heeded a voice, and the world was never the same. His name was Abraham—and what happened to him teaches us something profound about vision that Walt Disney somehow seemed to intuitively grasp.

When God Calls You to See Differently

> "The LORD had said to Abram, 'Go from your country, your people and your father's household to the land I will show you. I will make you into a great nation and I will bless you; I will make your name great, and you will be a blessing'" (Genesis 12:1-2).

Now, let's be honest for a second. If you had been Abraham, what would you have done with that message? I can imagine the conversation:

Abraham: "Um, excuse me, God? You want me to abandon everything I know, everyone I love, and go… where?"

2

God: "The land that I will show you."

Abraham: "Well, I understand that, but can you be more precise? Maybe a GPS coordinate? A general direction? North? South? A nice brochure with pictures? Can you tell me a bit more, I've got to take this info back to my wife."

But that's exactly the point. God didn't give Abraham a sixty-page business plan. He gave him a vision. He gave him a picture of something he could not boast about himself—becoming the father of nations and being a blessing to all the nations. He would fill in the details later. He would write the how-to booklet as he roamed. But the vision? The vision came first.

Abraham had to see it before he could be it.

Walt Disney knew how this worked—though what he had was not a vision of biblical proportions. When Walt first sat on that bench and had the first dreams of what would become Disneyland, he didn't have the money, he didn't have the land, he didn't even have the full support of some friends or some members of his own family. All he had was the vision.

For Abraham, Walt, and us, seeing the vision is the start, and as people of faith, we know it's the start of an incredible journey with God.

The Treasure Hunt of a Lifetime

Walt's road to realizing his dreams (in animation, as a studio boss, Disneyland, etc.) was not an easy one. The path was, in a sense, one failure after another—more failure than most people could endure. Today, Disney Parks are on both ends of America as well as in other places around the world. We sing their songs that we know by heart; we quote the dialogue of movies that we have watched a hundred times over. We wear the clothing. We eat Mickey head ice cream bars. And we may even own a few shares of their stock. But that was not always the case. There were many bumps in the road and times Walt Disney had more failures than successes.

When Walt was twenty-two, his first animation company, Laugh-O-Gram Studio, in Kansas City went bankrupt. He had started the studio in 1922 to produce modernized fairy tales, animated segments for the local theatre, and series of shorts that combined animation and live action. He also produced a dental hygiene film called "Tommy Tucker's Tooth" for a local dentist. However, by 1923, the studio was out of money. The cost of equipment, rent, and general overhead outpaced income. Out of sheer survival, Walt had run up a bill with the soft-hearted owner of a nearby restaurant to a point at which he couldn't charge food any longer. As the business continued to falter, Walt was so poor that he slept in his office, lived off cold beans straight from a can, and bathed at the local railroad station. He had no choice but to file bankruptcy, sell the majority of his equipment, and pay his investors pennies on the dollar.

Most people would have quit. The vast majority would have decided that the path they were on must not be their path. But here's the thing that separates visionary leaders from everyone else—visionary leaders know that failure is not the end, but just the opportunity to redirect. It's just a lesson that most of us, unfortunately, have to learn.

Walt believed in his vision—that he would lead an animation studio that would bring joy and magic to people. That meant that the setback (even a setback as big as bankruptcy) wasn't the end of the line. It was a time to think, reflect, and refocus.

One of the decisions that Walt made was that Kansas City wasn't where he needed to be. If he was going to produce cartoons and other shorts to be shown before the feature films in major theaters, then he needed to be where feature films were made. So, in 1923 (the same year that Laugh-O-Gram went bankrupt), Walt boarded a train for Hollywood. He had $40 in his pocket, his one other shirt and a change of underwear in his cardboard suitcase, and a first-class one-way ticket on the west-bound train. He had no firm plans, no offer of work, nothing solid to stand on, and yet, when someone on the train asked him why he was going to Hollywood—he told them he was going to be the head of an animation studio.

For visionary leaders, setbacks do not blind us to the vision, they help us focus.

Once in Hollywood, Walt partnered with his brother, Roy, in founding the Disney Brothers Studio. They produced a series of shorts that found a modest level of popularity, but in 1927, they developed their first star—Oswald the Lucky Rabbit. Oswald cartoons were shown before feature-films made by Universal Studios. Walt was finally seeing the vision become reality. However, as popular as Oswald was, and as much growth as his cartoons had brought to the Disney studio, the studio was still struggling financially. So, Walt and Roy decided that Walt needed to go to New York City to meet with their distributor to renegotiate their payment per cartoon as well as issues around royalties.

Walt and his wife, Lillian, went to New York, and Walt went to meet with Charles Mintz who was the distributor who linked Walt to Universal. Walt needed more money for the studio, but Mintz had other plans. Mintz had double-crossed Walt in the original partnership contract Walt had signed and had written the contract to his own advantage. So, when Walt went to meet with Mintz, he informed Walt that upon his return to California he would find that Mintz owned the rights to Oswald the Lucky Rabbit and if Walt didn't start essentially working for him to produce cartoons, he would lose Oswald, and Mintz had already signed away virtually all of Walt's animators (seventeen of his twenty). It was a blow that would have knocked most people down for the count. But not Walt.

Mintz thought that Walt would want to keep producing Oswald cartoons, and that he would not want to give up the guarantee of a salary, but Mintz underestimated the power of a vision. Walt's vision wasn't that he would one day work for someone he didn't respect just to get a check. Walt's vision was to lead an animation studio that brought joy and magic to families. So, Walt turned Mintz down and said goodbye to Oswald and his animators.

During times when the chips were down—when all seemed lost, and the darkness was closing in—Walt was aware that failure was merely an opportunity to pivot. So, because Walt didn't allow the issues to keep him down, when he and Lillian were on their train ride back to California, Mickey Mouse was born. It was not the drawing of Mickey that we know and love—that would come later—but on the train, the vision was born. In a sense, losing Oswald was not so much a loss for Walt as much as it was an opportunity to pivot. We need to develop that attitude in our lives as well.

Think of it this way—God may have bigger, more important plans or dreams for us, and sometimes He has to close one door to open another.

It was years later that Walt realized how, although losing Oswald had been hard, it actually steered his career toward something far greater. Without that setback, he may have just kept slogging away at Oswald instead of planting the seed for a character who would one day become the foundation of his empire (We will return to this story in the next chapter.).

Isn't this the way God frequently works in us, too? What we initially consider as a loss, is actually preparing us for something greater. What looks like failure is the lesson that makes us better and helps us become or do something greater than we imagined.

We see this in the call and story of Abraham and Sarah. God then called them to leave their own land (and that had to be hard and very scary), but not without making them a promise. Abraham began the journey knowing that God would make him the father of nations. In so doing, each step away from his comfort zone became one step closer to what he was meant to do with his life.

What is God calling you to do?
What kind of leader is God calling you to be?
What vision has God placed on your heart?

Vision Is Communication, Not Just Inspiration

Once you have the vision, that's only 50 percent of the battle. You then have to communicate it. You have to capture the hearts and minds of the people who will be involved. This is where Walt Disney was a pure genius and, far too often, many of today's leaders are missing out.

Today's leaders may use charts, studies of trends, a spread sheet or two, and a projection of potential profit margin to try to persuade other people that his or her vision is worthy of becoming reality. But that is trying to get people to understand a vision before they can see it. Walt did things differently. Walt rolled up his sleeves and painted a picture of a vision that was bigger—one big enough to overcome the odds—and he taught others that the impossible is really possible!

At one point in his career, Walt had a vision of making a full-length animated movie, and he had one subject in mind: Snow White and the Seven Dwarfs. No one had ever tried this, and no one believed it could be done. To do it, the animators would have to produce thousands of feet of animated film—one cell at a time. So, Walt had to ask himself: without real life examples, an abundance of data, and a riveting slideshow, how would he persuade them?

He acted out the entire movie for them.

One October night in 1934, he presented his animation staff with a half dollar each, sent them out to have a steak dinner, and asked them to return to the studio after they ate. When they arrived back at Disney's soundstage, there was Walt standing by himself, only one bare bulb illuminating the partially darkened stage.

For the next three or four hours, Walt re-enacted the complete story of Snow White. He accomplished this by becoming and channeling each character—from the Evil Queen to all Seven Dwarfs. When he did each character, he would give them a completely individualized voice and equally distinct actions as he went up and down the stage. The animators sat there virtually hypnotized watching a great hypnotist at work. Walt delivered a one-man show that absolutely mesmerized the audience.

At the conclusion of the show, Walt Disney said it loud and clear—he cast the vision: Snow White would be their (and the world's) first full-length feature cartoon, that they would change the world of animation forever, and that they would enchant viewers in a way that live action could never accomplish. He was confident, he was excited, he was all in—and because they could see and feel his enthusiasm, the animators were willing to sign on and followed where Walt led. As one animator would later confess: "We were just carried away. I would have climbed a mountain full of wildcats to do everything I could to make Snow White."[1]

When you share a vision—while charts and graphs may be needed or necessary—tell a story that creates pictures in people's minds. Help them see the "why" of your vision, and not just "what" you want to do. Show them the benefits, not just the features. Help them see how your vision resonates with their values and aspirations. And never forget that people don't merely invest in visions: they invest in the vision-caster. As someone in the role of vision-caster, your credibility and passion are as important as what you're bringing to the table.

Abraham also understood this principle. So, when he had received his vision from God, he did not make it a private concern. Instead, he passed it along to his family, sharing the joy and hope with everyone in his house. Each and every time he built an altar, each step he took toward the Promised Land, it was a way of saying: "I have seen something greater than all that this here-and-now world offers and I'm walking toward it."

Here's the beautiful part of both cases—neither Walt nor Abraham thought they could realize their vision alone. Just as Abraham was the father of nations through his offspring. Walt made his vision become reality through a bunch of talented artists and storytellers. Without a

---

[1] Disney animator quoted in "The way Walt Disney inspired his team to make 'Snow White' reveals his creative genius - and insane perfectionism," Business Insider India, September 20, 2015.

community, a vision is just a mirage. A vision backed and embraced by a community becomes reality.

Discovering Your God-Given Purpose

So, what does that mean for you or me? Whether you are leading two people or leading two thousand; whether you are launching a new company or launching the next chapter of your life's purpose, this principle doesn't change: vision is not optional. It's essential.

Hopefully you have been thinking about the questions you read earlier:

What is God calling you to do?
What kind of leader is God calling you to be?
What vision has God placed on your heart?

But how do you find/hear/see YOUR vision? How will you figure out if an idea is a word from God, a vision from your Father, or is it just a fading dream or some quickly passing cultural fad?

Let me give you a five-step format. I know it's worked for me—and I know it will work for you too:

Step One: Prayer and Listening: Before you can see, you must focus. Walt Disney would roam around his studio at night, and during those long walks he would spend time dreaming and reflecting. In the Old Testament, Abraham would build altars and spend time talking with God. For them and for us, vision often comes in the times of silence when we stop pushing to get an answer, and we start listening for one. Prayer and listening are the key. You + spending time with God. You + spending time with Scripture. You + being quiet so that you can listen when God speaks.

Step Two: Survey of Gifts and Circumstances: God doesn't ordinarily call you to something for which you are completely unprepared or unqualified (Yes, it can happen, but it's not the norm.). Often God has been preparing us much longer than we are aware. Walt was not a theme park pioneer by some whim of fate—he had been building up to it through his career of storytelling, technology development, and entertainment. Abraham was not an overnight father of faith. God had been preparing him to be a leader. So, what has God been preparing you for? What gifts do you possess? What ability or passion has been low-heat-simmering in your life that God might already be using—seeds sown and beginning to sprout? Make a list of gifts, abilities, passions, and joys. Also, think through and write down the places where you see God helping you grow, or where He may be stirring up your passion.

Step Three: Goal Setting with Faith Integration: When you have an impression of which way God may be leading, or you sense that he is pointing in a particular direction—then it's time to focus and begin to plan. This is when you begin developing specific, measurable goals—and you aren't afraid if they require faith to realize. Walt didn't want to simply produce cartoons, he wanted to entertain families. This was a vision that would take him down many paths to get there. Abraham wasn't setting out just to "travel and see the world," he was going to become the father of nations. Your goals should be so clear that they require movement in your life while also being large enough that you'll need God to help.

Step Four: Action Steps: If you have no action, then vision is a mere illusion. Abraham and Walt both got up out of their chair, and began making progress toward their goals, even though they had no idea what the finished picture would look like. The reality is that you do not need to know what is on the other side of the hill in order to take the first step toward it, but you do have to take the first step if you are ever going to reach the top of a hill. So, what is the first step, the second, the tenth, the thirtieth? They may have to be refined along the way, but they help you start forming the map that gets you where God is calling you to go. Make a list of steps (Sometimes this is the hardest part, but if you don't have a plan, you can't work the plan.).

Step Five: Continuous Realignment: Here's the good news—the steps you just listed may change in order or change completely. The truth is—we don't know what we don't know. So, as you begin to follow the steps to accomplish the vision—you may find that step one is really step three and there are two other steps needed to get you going. Realignment, addition, and deletion of steps always happen.

Also, the steps along the way may change because the vision may change. I know, you may think this is confusing or wrong, but here is reality—vision is not something you receive just once from heaven; it is an ongoing dialogue with God. Walt kept refining his vision—cartoons that started out as "shorts" became full-length films, television shows and specials, live-action films, Disneyland, and later there would be Walt Disney World and EPCOT. As time went by, Abraham's perception of God's promise became deeper and fuller. He stayed in relationship with God, and God kept leading him, calling him, and encouraging him. Your vision will grow and deepen as you grow and deepen. Your vision could change, it could clarify, it could crystalize. The vision God may give you today, when fulfilled, will lead you to God's vision for tomorrow.

When it comes to vision—we never arrive. The blessing of fulfilling God's vision is that God will give us another vision, and then another, and then another.

Building a Culture of Visionary Thinking

Whether you lead a family, team, department, or company, you can create an atmosphere where it is natural and easy for vision to flourish. Walt Disney didn't just have a vision—he created an environment in which the entire team could catch and contribute to the vision.

How did he do it, and how can you do it too?

Make Vision Conversation, Not Presentation: Walt never delivered his vision in a boring or sterile way. He would share the vision in conversations, in one-on-one interactions, and (if to a group) in the most captivating way possible (remember he acted out all of *Snow White*). His favorite question was, "What if?" He would use that question to start a conversation and to invite people to think alongside him. His "What if?" questions would challenge his team to think new thoughts and to embrace new possibilities. What if animation were to achieve the same emotional depth as live-action films? What if we can make our own big-screen stories into a physical reality where entire families come right in and experience the joy for days and weeks on end? Questions that start with "What if" are seeds for possibility. These questions invite ideas and participation. Statements create distance and separation.

Celebrate Small Steps Toward Big Visions: Every achievement at Disney—sound synchronization, Technicolor, feature length animation, multiplane photography for real depth backgrounds—were all celebrated as steppingstones toward Walt's bigger vision. In the Bible, Abraham "rejoiced to see" and celebrate each time a promise was realized. He interpreted every development as proof that God was continuing to steer him in the direction of His ultimate goal. As we are casting vision, and leading vision—there is no reason to wait before we let people celebrate the vision. As leaders, we need to realize and rejoice over the small improvements being made on each step of the journey.

Encourage "What If" Thinking: As I previously mentioned, Walt's favorite question was "What if?" What if we could make a mouse talk? What if we could make a cartoon that was as emotionally engaging as a live-action film? What if we constructed a place where dreams become real? "What if" opens new possibilities. When we surrender ourselves to God, who is still able to do something miraculous with our lives, it creates new opportunities for his grace and power. "What if" questions open minds to what might be, and they provide space for God to enact something new. What are the "what if" questions you need to share with others to engage them in your vision? What are the "what if" questions you need to ask to help others open up to what God wants to do?

The Vision That Changes Everything

Here's the reality that Walt and Abraham finally arrived at: when you link your dream to a larger vision, it will become bigger than you. And, it has the power to bless not only you, but everyone who comes near it. After all, Abraham didn't just want to enrich himself personally. His vision included blessing the entire earth. Walt didn't envision simply making money for himself in the entertainment industry. It was much bigger than that. Walt's goal was to keep families connected and transform them with memories that would last forever—moments of joy and magic.

What's your vision? Not just the goals you've set for your own life and the income gap you'd like to bridge. What sort of world do you want to build? What is it that you want to be remembered for? What's the blessing God desires to do in and through your life?

If you don't yet know, that is okay. When Abraham first heard the call of God, he had no idea all that God was going to do through him. When Walt sketched Mickey Mouse on that train, he didn't know the little mouse would become a global icon (On the train, Mickey didn't look like our idea of the mouse we know and love—he looked more like a rat. And his name was Mortimer until Lillian revised it to Mickey.). Vision frequently begins with just an idea, or a murmur, a sketch or a doodle, or a small thought in the back of your mind: and you think, "What if there's something more?"

Here is something I've learned from some of history's great leaders:

- Your vision will shape the size of your life.
- Small visions make small lives.
- But big, God-sized visions create big, God-sized impact.

Faith and Life Application: Vision As Partnership with God

When you have vision, it changes everything about how you approach every day of your life and leadership. Instead of just doing something, you're getting somewhere. You are not reacting to the situation, but you are generating circumstances that flow with God's plans and purposes.

When you wake up in the morning, answer the question: "What action step can I take today that would point me toward the vision God gave me?" Perhaps it's a conversation you should have, or a skill you should build, or a prayer you need to pray. No matter what the step, take it!

Remember, God doesn't just call the qualified—He qualifies those He calls. Was Abraham prepared to become the father of nations when God initially called him? Not likely. On the secular side—when Walt had a few sketches and dreams, was he poised to change how we view entertainment? No way. As both men were faithful their purpose became clearer as they moved toward the vision that had been cast.

Your vision may seem impossible right now. Good! That's to say it's large enough that it requires God. That means it's worth your life. That means, when it happens, everybody will know it was not just because of human effort, but it was done in partnership with heaven itself.

Leadership Application: Communicating Vision That Captures Hearts

When you're leading the way, your ability to cast vision may be your most important skill to develop. After all, people don't follow managers; they follow visionary leaders. People don't give their best effort on assignments; they bring their energies and their attention to causes and visions they believe in.

Here are the basics in terms of communicating a vision that inspires people to action:

Start with Why, Not What – Don't lead with all the things you want people to do. Begin with why it matters. The people you lead (or hope to lead) must hear from your heart why your vision matters. Walt didn't say, "I want to build an amusement park, and here are the many tasks I want you to do." He said, "I [feel] that there should be something built where the parents and the children could have fun together."[2] The vision wasn't another park with an old carousel, it was a vision of a transformative family experience.

Use Stories, Not Numbers – Numbers inform the mind; stories move the heart. Walt didn't try to convince his people with market research; he told the story of *Snow White* and won them over. Testimonies, case studies, and personal experience are the "data" that should be shared to help people see what might be—these will inspire far more than merely statistical research.

Invite Participation, Not Just Compliance – The best visions are not monologues or one-way streets—they are achieved through teamwork. Ask your team: "How do you see yourself contributing to this vision?" "What are some ideas that would make this better?" "What are the barriers you think we need to overcome together?" When people help shape the vision, they own it.

Connect Vision to Values – Your vision should be a direct extension of your organization's deepest values, and your vision should be the embodiment of WHAT YOU VALUE. If your values are excellence and integrity, your vision should reflect those

---

[2] Walt Disney, archival footage, ABC News' "The Happiest Story on Earth: 70 Years of Disneyland – 20/20 Special Edition," September 2025.

qualities. If your values include serving others and bringing glory to God, your vision must move them forward. When vision and values are in sync, you have authenticity. When they conflict, you sow confusion. What are your deepest values?

Repeat, Repeat, Repeat – Vision leaks. People forget. Circumstances change. Communication is not a closing argument—it's a conversation. Walt talked about his vision for Disneyland for years before building it. It took decades for Abraham's vision of a homeland to be realized. Keep the vision in front of people, through every possible channel, always.

The world needs leaders who see beyond the status quo to the potential of what could be. The world needs leaders who are in partnership with God and are working to bring His Kingdom purposes to life on earth. The world needs leaders who comprehend that vision isn't just about creating something successful—it's about creating something significant.

You could be one of those leaders. It's not a question of whether you are capable or prepared. The question is, do you have the guts to look beyond where you are at this moment and see what God wants to do in your life?

The vision is out there, waiting to be discovered. The question is: Are you ready to see it?

CHAPTER TWO

The Foundation That Never Fails

Faith and Trust

In the last chapter, I mentioned the story from March of 1928, when Walt and Lillian made the journey from California to New York City. Walt was out there for what he thought would be a routine contract negotiation with Charles Mintz, who distributed Walt's cartoons with Universal Studios. Instead, Walt lost everything.

Oswald the Lucky Rabbit was the creation of Disney Brothers Studio. He was their first hit, and his success had caused the studio to expand and Walt to feel like his vision was becoming a reality. But Walt hadn't fully read the distribution contract because he trusted Mintz and, unfortunately, he had indeed signed away the rights to his creation.

Walt came to New York expecting to haggle terms that would yield him higher revenue for his studio but found himself staring financial ruin in the face. At the end of their meeting, Walt opted to just walk away from the contract with Mintz because he knew he would never achieve his vision if his future was controlled by someone like Mintz.

As Walt and Lillian packed their bags for departure from New York City, Walt realized that he needed to share the news with his brother and business partner, Roy. However, instead of sending Roy a telegram filled with doom and gloom, Walt wired: "LEAVING TONIGHT STOPPING OVER KC ARRIVE HOME SUNDAY MORNING SEVEN THIRTY DON'T WORRY EVERYTHING OK WILL GIVE DETAILS WHEN ARRIVE – WALT."[3]

Think about that for a moment. Walt had just been wiped out, but his message was one of confidence and possibility. That wasn't denial—that was leadership. Walt was well aware that leaders need to be thermostats rather than thermometers. They are called to set the temperature rather than just reflecting it.

As that train made its way to Kansas City for Walt and Lillian to visit family and then on to California, Walt was thinking about what new opportunity was next. He started to sketch (something that he no longer did very often), and a little mouse called Mortimer emerged. He basically looked like a pointy nosed rat. Little did he know that this scribbled sketch, conceived in his darkest professional moment, would lay the groundwork for a global industry. Once one of his remaining animators, Ub Iwerks, took Walt's drawing and directions, and Lillian had given him a less pretentious name—Mickey Mouse was born.

---

[3] Walt Disney telegram to Roy Disney, March 1928, as documented in multiple Disney biographies including Neal Gabler's *Walt Disney: The Triumph of the American Imagination* and various Disney historical archives.

On the train, where the world would have said "all is lost," Walt was looking forward. He didn't know what was next. He didn't have a business plan. He didn't have well thought out market research. He didn't even have money. But what he did have was far more powerful—faith.

Of course, I know some of you are thinking: "Great story, but he didn't know that the sketch of a rat would be a success and faith doesn't pay the mortgage." And you're right—faith doesn't write the checks. But here's what I've found after decades of watching leaders rise and fall like stock prices in a volatile market: the leaders who build something lasting aren't necessarily the smartest or the most talented. They are the ones who know that lasting significance cannot be built on anything other than a solid foundation of faith in their vision—a foundation that can weather any storm.

FYI—In 2006, Disney's CEO Bob Iger negotiated an unusual deal with NBC Universal. Disney released Al Michaels from his contract with ESPN/ABC so he could sign with NBC Universal. In return, NBC Universal gave Oswald the Lucky Rabbit back to Disney.

The Faith That Moves Mountains (and Mice)

Faith is not only a religious word—faith is also a leadership imperative. I don't mean the blind kind of faith where you leap off a cliff and hope that you will grow wings on the way down. That usually ends badly and suddenly. I mean that Christian leaders have the kind of faith that says, "I don't have all the answers, but I know Who does, so I'm going to take the next right step."

Walt Disney had an instinctive gift for this. Even after the Oswald disaster, he didn't become embittered or give up on his vision. Rather, he did what all great leaders do when they find themselves in a hopeless situation: he trusted that his talents and abilities were not given to him accidentally, but for a purpose. So, he got back to work.

When you read the Old Testament, you find another leader who had overwhelming odds stacked against him—a young shepherd boy named David. Let me assure you—I am not going to retell the WHOLE David and Goliath story (you probably heard it in Sunday school, and trust me, the flannel board version was probably more dramatic than most Hollywood movies). But there's one thing about David's approach that every Christian leader needs to understand.

When David presented himself to King Saul as the warrior to face Goliath, Saul attempted to have him fitted in royal armor. The armor was impressive, expensive, and had probably been made by the best military minds of the day. There was just one hitch: it didn't fit David. The Bible tells us that David "tried walking around" in Saul's armor, but he removed it and said, essentially, "Thanks, but no thanks. I'll stick with what I know works."

David stepped up and confronted a nine-foot giant with a sling, five smooth stones, and steadfast faith in the God who had previously helped him kill lions and bears while protecting his father's sheep. From a purely tactical perspective, this was an awful strategy. From a faith stand-point, it was genius.

Now, you may be thinking, "Well, if he had faith, why did he take five smooth stones to fight Goliath? Wouldn't it show more faith to only take one?" I suppose that would be right—EXCEPT—Goliath had four brothers. So, when David killed Goliath with the first stone, he was prepared if the other four decided to retaliate.

When the Armor Doesn't Fit

Here's the thing I love about both David and Walt Disney: they understood that true leadership arises from genuine faith. David's story would have had a different meaning and feel if he would have worn Saul's armor and pretended to be something that he wasn't. Walt could have walked away from animation and pursued a "safer" career (while his brother, Roy, partnered with Walt, their brother Herbert worked as a mail carrier, and their other brother Raymond sold insurance), but he'd have spent the rest of his life asking himself one question: What if?

Too many Christian leaders today are attempting to dress themselves in Saul's armor. They are trying to lead using someone else's tactics, someone else's vision, some-one else's faith. They've believed the lie that being a good leader is imitating someone else's leadership style that seemed to work, rather than trusting God—who is the one who placed them in their role and gave them their opportunities.

Walt Disney's faith wasn't complicated. He believed that good things would come if he worked hard, treated people fairly, and never skimped on quality. That's not naive optimism—that's biblical wisdom in practice. The Bible instructs "in all thy ways acknowledge Him, and He shall direct your paths" (Proverbs 3:6). Walt may not have quoted that verse, but he embodied it.

Shortly after the Mickey Mouse cartoons started catching on, Walt's faith was once again tested. The Great Depression hit, and it seemed like his entertainment business was doomed. Food, not to mention movie tickets, was beyond everybody's means. Walt's advisers told him to cut costs by reducing the quality of his animated shorts. "Give people what they can afford," they said.

But Walt took a gamble that became the signature of his entire career: he bet on the idea that quality will always find its following. Instead of slashing corners, he invested even more time and money making his cartoons better. He brought in color animation even though everyone told him it was too expensive. He created elaborate storylines when everyone kept saying cartoons should be simple. He believed that if he made something exceptional, people would figure out a way to experience it.

Building on the Rock

Remember the parable Jesus shared about the wise man who built his house on a rock and the foolish man who built his house on sand (Matthew 7:24-27)? Because of how houses were built in that part of the world in the first century, I would think that the two houses looked pretty similar. The difference showed up when the storms arrived.

Walt wasn't the only studio head who made cartoon shorts—there were many. And they were all around the same length and produced through a similar process. However, Walt built his career on a few unshakeable beliefs: the pursuit of excellence, the importance of honesty, the value of creativity, and the conviction that his work really mattered. When the storms hit—and boy did they hit—those principles formed a foundation that allowed him to keep moving forward toward his goals.

Think about the making of Snow White and the Seven Dwarfs. This was not just Disney's first feature-length animated film; it was the first feature-length animated film ever made. The entire entertainment industry called it "Disney's Folly." They insisted that audiences wouldn't sit through a full-length cartoon. Some critics said that IF anyone watched a full-length animated movie—they would go insane. They said a feature-length animated movie would bankrupt the company. They said Walt had finally lost his mind.

How did Walt respond? Walt mortgaged his house, took loans against future earnings, and put every resource he had into this project. Why? Because he believed—in the project, yes, but also in the vision. He was motivated to push the envelope of what was possible in the world of entertainment.

While making Snow White, at times, Walt was unable to pay his animators. So, instead of laying them off, he brought them together and showed them what they were building. He painted the vision of what this film could be—not just for Disney Studios, but for the whole entertainment and animation business. He urged them to have faith in him, to believe in this once-in-a-lifetime crusade, and trust that the sacrifice would be worth it.

And you know what happened? Many of the animators worked without pay for months, driven by little more than the infectious spirit of Walt and a camaraderie that convinced them they could create something the world had never seen before.

The Faith Factor in Leadership

This brings me to a fundamental principle of leadership that all Christian leaders need to know—your level of faith will affect the level of faith in your team. People don't rally behind someone who is unsure and second guesses themselves. People follow leaders who have clear visions and an unstoppable faith that the vision can and should be realized.

But this is the distinction between worldly confidence and biblical faith: worldly confidence relies upon circumstances, resources, and probabilities. Biblical faith originates from the nature of God and the calling He has placed on you.

When Moses found himself before the Red Sea and with Pharaoh's army riding down hard behind him, he didn't try to engineer a plan B. He anchored his faith in his belief that the God who called him to lead His people out of Egypt would not leave them hanging when it mattered most. And when Moses held out his staff over the sea, God divided the water.

Walt Disney had a Red Sea moment of his own in the construction of Disneyland. The park was scheduled to open in July 1955, but as the date approached absolutely nothing seemed to be complete. It was clear to everyone who was building each land and attraction: The park wasn't ready for visitors. The asphalt was still wet, most of the rides were not yet up and running, and gas leaks were scattered throughout the park. Everyone was telling Walt to push the opening back.

But Walt had a deal with the television network that was broadcasting the opening ceremony live to millions of Americans. He'd even nailed down some celebrity pals to preside over the telecast opening: Art Linkletter, Bob Cummings, and Ronald Reagan (Yeah, that one. Don't forget, he was an actor first). And most importantly, Walt had told the American public that Disneyland would open July 17, 1955. So, he wouldn't delay.

That first day was, as the world knows, a disaster by most estimates and is still dubbed "Black Sunday." The asphalt was so scorching hot that women in high heels were finding themselves stuck in it. Several attractions broke down on live television. There were traffic jams that lasted hours. Folks had made their own tickets and were climbing the walls—so all of the rides and food sources were completely overwhelmed. And poor Walt. He almost missed it all because the freshly painted door to his apartment over the Fire Station dried shut—temporarily trapping him until someone helped break it open. But Walt never gave up hope; after all, he knew that Disneyland was not just another amusement park—it reflected his wildest dreams and highest vision of a world filled with wonder and joy that families could experience together.

When journalists asked Walt about the park's issues and whether it should have been delayed from opening, his signature glass-half-full reply was: "I don't expect the place will ever be finished. That's what I like about it. That it will always be growing."[4] Walt did not allow himself to become enveloped in what went wrong; he kept thinking about what could be done better.

Faith Without Works Is Dead

I do not believe that faith is going to God in prayer and then just sitting back waiting for some miracle to happen. Faith, in the biblical sense, always demands action. James 2:17 says that "faith, if it doesn't have works, is dead."

Walt Disney's faith in his vision was an active one. It wasn't so much that he believed good things would happen—he knew that he had to help make them happen. He spent long hours practicing his craft, studying the kinds of things that his audiences liked, and pushing himself to do new things. Sometimes he expanded boundaries, and sometimes he completely blew through them. His faith gave him the courage to take a risk, but it was his work ethic that was the substance of his faith.

---

[4] Walt Disney, quoted by reporters, July 17, 1955, Disneyland opening day, as documented in "'Black Sunday': Remembering Disneyland's disastrous opening day," SFGate, July 17, 2022.

Here's where a lot of Christian leaders get confused. They believe faith means that God does everything. Or they think success means doing everything themselves without God. However, the examples we find in the Bible teach us that we are called to be both totally dependent on God and giving our best work to God every day.

Let me share with you one of my favorite stories from the Old Testament, a story about Nehemiah, who rebuilt the wall around Jerusalem. When Nehemiah discovered that the walls of Jerusalem had been destroyed, he did more than pray (although he did spend four months praying a whole lot). He worked out a plan, a process, a strategy. He collected the resources necessary, then organized people to help with the work. He cast the vision and rallied people around it—then he stepped out and led by example. It was his faith that gave him vision and courage to attempt the impossible. It was his grit that brought the vision to life.

Nehemiah had enemies coming at him from all sides. Sanballat, the governor of Samaria and Tobiah the Transjordan provincial official both mocked the project and threatened to attack and disrupt. Even some of Nehemiah's own people grumbled at the workload. There was little in the way of resources, and the work was risky. But Nehemiah's response to opposition reveals the secret to faith-based leadership, "We prayed to our God and posted a guard day and night to meet this threat" (Nehemiah 4:9). They prayed—and they kept working.

Pray and post a guard. Put your full trust in God and be diligent in what He's called you to do. Trust in the plan and take your role in seeing it come to fruition.

When Faith Meets Failure

Of course, faith doesn't mean it's all going to be easy. Walt Disney had faced a string of failures during his career. His first animation studio went bankrupt. Some of his films initially bombed at the box office. The opening day of Disneyland was a public relations disaster. But Walt knew something that every Christian leader needs to learn:

Failure is not the opposite of faith—frequently it's faith's most effective teacher.

In the Bible, so many times leaders experience a setback on a massive scale just prior to breakthrough. Joseph was sold into slavery and ended up in prison before he rose to become second to the Pharaoh of Egypt. Moses worked forty years in the land of Midian before he brought the children of Israel out from bondage. It took David years of running from King Saul before he became king himself.

In each case, the setback wasn't the end of the story—it was preparation for the next chapter. It was not that faith delivered them from troubles, but it steered them through their troubles and turned their setbacks into setups for something better.

Building a Faith-Based Team

When I think about Walt's leadership—one of the qualities that is most extraordinary was his ability to encourage others to share his faith and vision in seemingly impossible dreams. It wasn't that he was a slick talker, or a master manipulator. It was the reality, and contagion, of his own faith that made people unable to help but believe along with him.

When Walt had the vision to create Disneyland, he didn't just require money; he required believers in that dream, and they turned up in the most unexpected places. He gathered a team of artists, engineers, architects, and storytellers who had never worked together before, and convinced them that they could actually make something the world had not yet seen.

This is a little like how, in the Bible, Jesus called His disciples. It wasn't the religious elite he chose; it wasn't the pros. He chose fishermen and a tax collector—ordinary folks who were open to believing in something extraordinary. It wasn't their competence that made them effective; it was their willingness to surrender themselves to Jesus' vision and follow him.

That is the challenge of Christian leaders today. We must form teams of those who not only share our vision but also share our faith that the vision can be achieved. This requires several key elements:

First, **transparency about the challenges**. Walt was always upfront with his team about how difficult a battle it would be. He did not sugarcoat the financial risks or the technical challenges. But he paired realism about the problems with faith in the possibilities. Jesus shared with the disciples in the Sermon on the Mount—His first message to them after they were called—that people were going to reject and abuse them because of Him. However, if they were faithful—theirs would be the Kingdom of Heaven.

Second, **clarity about the purpose**. People will suffer and sacrifice when they know their labor has a point. Walt consistently communicated that they weren't just making movies, they weren't simply building a theme park, but, rather, they were bringing joy and magic to families around the world. Jesus reminded His disciples that when they ministered in His name, the Kingdom of God was coming near to people—that is life changing and even world changing.

Third, **consistency in character**. Faith-based teams require faith-based leaders. People are watching to see if our deeds are consistent with our words, if we're really what we appear to be in our private lives and in our public ideals. People notice if our vision, our faith, and our beliefs hold up when the pressure is on. Unfortunately, some leaders cast visions that are simply based on the need to be popular or fit in with the culture around them—the vision isn't rooted in who they are and who God has called them to be. Typically, that vision shifts frequently when the wind of cultural trend blows a different direction. This makes it even more important for Christian leaders to root their leadership in their faith and their vision in the God who never changes.

The Compound Effect of Faith

Here is something interesting about faith: it compounds over time. Walt Disney's early hits with Mickey Mouse allowed him the momentum to dream about Snow White. The Silly Symphonies provided him with the skills necessary to make Snow White. The success of Snow White paved the way for him to dream big dreams about Disneyland. The success of Disneyland allowed him to envision a place like EPCOT. Each leap of faith and each decision to trust instead of worry allowed him to keep building and growing closer to his vision.

This is why the Bible speaks of "going from faith to faith" (Romans 1:17). Our faith is developed through exercise; in the same way our muscles grow when used. Every time we choose to believe in God instead of what we see, every time our actions are shaped by His promises rather than reaction to our fears, we're building our faith capacity for the next step.

It's a phenomenon I've seen countless times in the lives of Christian leaders. The pastor who takes a small church, and works faithfully to follow God's will, and over time the church grows—then the pastor gets the opportunity to serve a larger church. The executive who does a small deal with integrity is developing the character necessary to pursue larger deals. The leader who serves faithfully over smaller tasks learns how to lead in more significant ways.

This is something Walt Disney fully understood. He never tried to jump through the stages of preparation or attempted to avoid them. Every beast to be faced, every limit to be pushed, and every adventure to venture provided him with the lessons he needed to learn—small steps and choices made along the way. Each of those victories (or losses) gave him permission to take on something more ambitious.

Faith and Innovation

One very clear connection between Walt Disney and some of the larger-than-life leaders in the Bible was the willingness to take the risk to be innovative, to discover new ways of doing things, to put themselves out on a limb, and even fail in order to accomplish something bigger or better. It is always a leap of faith because it's always going into the unknown.

Making cartoons was nice, but Walt wanted to revolutionize what animation was and unlock its potential. He wasn't simply going to open an amusement park—he was out to invent an entirely new form of family entertainment. Both of these forced him to push himself beyond his comfort zone, and what he already knew. He could have done things the "safe way," but playing it safe would never get him where he wanted to go.

Consider King David again. He beat Goliath... not with conventional weapons. On the field of battle, he innovated and used his God-given talents and skills in ways that no one saw coming or expected to work. The result was—the risk paid off—David won. His willingness to take the risk, to do it his way, to think outside the box gave him a reputation as a leader and inspired his country.

Innovation is always an act of faith, because it means doing something that isn't certain, and you can't guarantee will work. If we want to be leaders, we have to be willing to take that leap of faith and trust that God has placed within us the ability and means to move forward toward our vision—even if it's not yet clear how that's possible.

As leaders we must realize that what was good enough for your mom's and grandmom's generations won't work now. The world is always changing. Even the most traditional and staid professions must learn to adapt. Therefore, we need to be able to have the faith to try new tactics, while refusing to give up on older principles or to compromise our values.

In the Bible this is referred to as not putting new wine in old wineskins. Old wineskins are probably brittle and won't be able to expand to allow the new wine to ferment. You put new wine in new wineskins, then as it's fermenting, expanding, and becoming what it was meant to become, the wineskin expands and adapts to accommodate. It's still wine—red, white, sweet, dry—it hasn't changed its principles or values—it just needs the space to grow and become the best it can be.

Walt Disney's readiness to take a gamble was not risk for risk's sake; it was faith-based risk. He learned his craft with a particular rigor, and he always surrounded himself with talented people. This meant that he had the faith to make decisions and take risks based on sound principles, core values, and quality advice. Therefore, he never feared to venture into uncharted territory because he had this belief that excellence and integrity would ultimately be recognized and rewarded. And he was always willing to move from the old wineskins (the old way of doing things—the established traditional ways) and make new wineskins (new technology, new markets, new methods) to continue moving toward his vision.

The Legacy of Faith

When I am writing these words Walt Disney has been gone nearly sixty years and yet his presence is only expanding. His company is one of the best-known brands on earth. The characters he created still delight children—and, let's be honest, adults too—on every continent. The theme parks he dreamed up still attract millions of visitors each year.

The thing that most impresses me about Walt's legacy, though, is that it's not just about entertainment. It's about how vision-based leadership can achieve something that outlasts our own lives. Walt reminded us that if we allow our vision and faith to lead us and continue to lift others up as we journey toward our goal… then long after we're gone, people will still be benefiting from the seeds we planted.

This is what any Christian leader should want to leave behind as a legacy. Not just success for one season, but impact that lives on through the generations. Not simply achievement that brings glory or recognition to us, but influence which leads others to God.

The Bible says, "The righteous will be remembered forever" (Psalm 112:6). Which isn't, of course, fame or recognition in any worldly sense. It's hinting at the ripple effects of a life lived in faith, the enduring impact of decisions made in light of eternity, and an ongoing generational heritage that reflects the heart of God.

Walt Disney was not a pastor or missionary, but his life does reflect, in its own way, biblical truth. His faith in his vision challenged an entire industry to strive higher. His lifelong contribution to family-friendly entertainment provided a moral alternative at times when society seemed to be in free fall. I know that his willingness to dream big has inspired many others who have gone on to accomplish their God-given dreams.

Faith in Action: Personal Application

So how do we connect these principles to our leadership journey? How do we develop the faith that enables us to persevere through disappointments and to accomplish the remarkable?

First, **start with your foundation**. What foundation does your leadership stand on? Is it built on your talents and abilities or is it God's nature and call? Have you put on someone else's armor or are you leading from your real identity, faith, values, and integrity?

Take a step back and honestly evaluate the way in which you lead today. Are your decisions made from a place of fear or faith? Are you fixated on what you don't have, or are you grateful for everything that God's blessed you with? Are you always attempting to control the results or are you wisely stewarding what is under your control and trusting God with everything else?

Second, **clarify your calling**. Walt Disney had a laser focus on what he was meant to do. He wasn't trying to please all the people all the time; he simply wanted family-friendly entertainment that would bring joy to people and deliver a little magic into their lives. What is God asking you to create, to lead, to influence? Are you focused? Or do you chase after every "new thing" that pops into your mind?

You may not feel like you're called to build a global entertainment empire, but your calling is no less important. Whether you are managing a business, church ministry, nonprofit organization, or the family in which God has given you a realm of influence. Whatever it is, wherever it is, what does He want you to build?

Third, **commit to excellence**. Faith-led vision that isn't striving for excellence is simply wrong. Faith-led leadership should NEVER settle for mediocrity. Walt Disney's achievements achieved a lasting legacy because he always brought his vision to life by demanding excellence in every last detail. He even had a practice he called "plussing" where he would strive to add greater value to everything. He always wanted to do more than was expected and give more than necessary. How are you embodying excellence in your work habits, in every role you play, or do you settle for "good enough" when it's never REALLY good enough.

Excellence is not perfectionism or workaholism. It is doing your very best work as an offering to God. It is constantly and consistently learning more and growing more—all the time—and never settling when you should be striving.

Fourth, **build your faith capacity**. Just like we need to exercise physically, we must exercise our faith if we want it to grow. What are you doing to deliberately nourish your faith? Would you accept challenges that require you to trust God more? Is your environment filled with people who build your faith or people who feed your fears?

Start a faith journal—jot down how God shows up in your journey as a leader. Write down the moments you experience Him showing up with what you didn't have, opening doors which YOU couldn't open, and giving wisdom beyond what you knew. One day this account will be a powerful testimony of the faithfulness of God, and it WILL strengthen your faith to face whatever lies ahead.

Faith in Action: Leadership Application

Now, let's talk about how all of this applies directly to Christian leadership as it plays out in your life today:

The development of a faith-based organizational culture starts with you as a leader making faith-based decisions. Your team is watching to see how you perform when the things are tight, tensions are high, resources are limited, deadlines are short, and criticism is plentiful. Do you lose control and micromanage, or do you stand strong and believe in the sovereignty of the Lord? Do you abandon your principles for convenience—or do you stand by them, come what may?

Walt Disney's employees bought what he was selling because they could look in his eyes and see that he'd never give up on the vision, however tempting it might have been at times. Certainly, as Christian leaders, we should have more consistency and backbone than everyone else if our lives and our leadership are built on the solid foundation of faith.

Let your faith be demonstrated in the way you lead, not just by the things you say. Christian leaders should possess certain key qualities:

- They are not afraid under pressure because they remember that God is still in charge.
- They base decisions on principles not pragmatism.
- They invest in their people because they believe in human potential.
- They are willing to take risks because they know that God is with them.
- They are people who endure setbacks because they see the bigger picture.

Build systems that reflect your faith. This could range from hiring practices that prioritize character in addition to competence, or a policy of maintaining the health and welfare of employees even when it is not economical, or even strategic choices that put long-term effect ahead of short-term gain.

Walt Disney chose to operate with systems that reflected his values: prioritizing a great storytelling experience over rushing to save money, pouring resources into developing and training his people, and reinvesting profit in the form of new innovations when other executives might have doubled down on maximizing short-term financial returns.

Develop other faith-based leaders. One of Walt's most significant legacies is the leaders he helped to create along his journey. He poured into his top employees, and the result was that several of them later headed major projects or started successful companies themselves. They were shaped by the lessons and values they had absorbed from him.

Christian leaders could learn from this. Each of us should be helping to make the leaders of tomorrow by being their "lead-investor." Our goal should be to help develop them into leaders who lead with faith and who have the integrity to make faith-led decisions. That's the multiplier effect that makes a lasting impact for generations.

Make decisions from a legacy perspective. Walt Disney always seemed to think in long-term truths, asking himself how history would regard his choices. That long view is what allowed him to choose quality over convenience and durable values over cheap profits.

Christian leaders should ask those same questions: "What does this decision say to others about the character of God?" "What example am I setting for young leaders... those who are going to come behind me?" "Will what I'm building bring glory to God and good to others long after I am gone?"

The Faith Journey Continues

You will never find yourself accidentally becoming a faith-based leader. It is a journey you must choose. One thing I have discovered is there will always be mountains that require us to go higher and will require greater faith; opportunities that will push us to trust God in deeper ways, and seasons where we are reminded of how important it is to renew our commitment to live faithfully for God every day and in every decision.

Walt Disney understood this. He kept taking chances even after he became monstrously successful, assuming that his best work was always before him. When he passed away, he had not only been working on the development of what would be Walt Disney World, he had also been working on the plans for EPCOT. He was always envisioning new opportunities to bring service to his guests, to inspire families, and give them magic and memories.

It is the same forward-looking faith that we, as Christian leaders, must maintain. Yesterday's victories prepare us for whatever tomorrow brings, but they do not exempt us from the necessity of trusting God in the future.

The firm anchor of faith that shapes extraordinary leadership doesn't develop overnight. Instead, it is cultivated through big and small moments strung together over the span of our life. Those moments when we determine to trust God's character when things don't make sense, to rely on His promises instead of obsessing over our problems and adhere to His timeline rather than surrendering to our sense of urgency.

The legacy of Walt Disney is a reminder that if we continue to build our vision on the foundation of faith, reach for new heights, and maintain integrity in our relationships with others, we can leave something lasting. Better still, Scripture teaches us that when we lead in such a way as to establish harmony and agreement between our leadership and God's own heart and purposes, we ourselves get to participate in the kingdom work of God, which will have eternal significance.

The question here isn't that you don't have enough faith to lead well. The question is: are you going to be someone who acts on the measure of faith God has given you, trusting Him to multiply your offering as His Holy Spirit leads and opens doors for you?

As we go forward, we will explore how faith translates into the courage that is necessary for breakthrough leadership. The kind of courage that inspires everyday people to do something out-of-the-ordinary for God's glory. So, let me leave you with a simple fact for now. If Walt Disney can have a dream of bringing joy and magic into the lives of families and see that dream become a reality, then you can trust that God can give you a vision for your world. But do you have the faith to pursue it?

CHAPTER THREE

The Courage to Color Outside the Lines

Courage and Risk-taking

When we are talking about Walt Disney and "courage and risk-taking" then the conversation must circle back to "Disney's Folly." As we looked at earlier, in 1937, Walt Disney was determined to do the impossible. He set out to do something that many in the entertainment industry felt was a foolish waste of time and money. He mortgaged his house, and borrowed against his life insurance, but the reality was he would do anything he had to do to finance this gamble. He knew that the next step in accomplishing his vision was a full-length animated film that told the story of a young lady living with seven small men in a forest (AKA Snow White and the Seven Dwarfs).

Walt's commitment to this project was because he had seen something very few were able to see. He saw animation as a way into the greater world of storytelling. He felt that it could be equally capable of making an audience cry or laugh—or both. He knew in his heart that good storytelling would trump whatever the medium, and that all people would care about were the characters and the story—regardless of whether it was live action or animation.

And so, Walt did what courageous leaders do: He risked everything for his dream.

I am going to pause here for something… because some of you are already thinking what every person on the planet says when I tell this story, and that is: "That's not courage—that's just crazy!" Trust me, I understand the confusion. As a leader who has been leading for a while, I can tell you, the line you walk between courage and stupidity is sometimes skinnier than the storyline in a bad rom-com.

But know that there is a difference between courage and stupidity. Stupidity acts without preparation or thought. Courage acts in spite of whatever fear is felt because it can trust in the steps that have gotten it there, and it acts in accordance with the principles, values, and faith that have been its foundation. Walt Disney wasn't gambling with his own fate or that of his company, he had faith that he was setting the stage to accomplish the vision that had guided him for years. And Walt firmly believed that, though he couldn't see or understand it at the time—everything he had experienced—good and bad, success and failure—had been preparing him for this moment in time.

Once, when I was leading a trip to England and Ireland, I was standing in the Tube in London. The subway car was fairly empty when my group got on board. However, stop after stop people got on, and no one seemed to get off. The car was filling up fast, and after three to four stops it was cramped and crowded. Suddenly, people were pressed up against me—one from my group and the rest were strangers. The one from my group knew that I do not like anyone "friend or foe" entering my personal space, but there they all were. So, he leaned in and, in his most ominous voice at a volume only I could hear, said, "Everything you have ever done or not done—every decision you have ever made or delayed—it has all led you to this moment in time—this group of people that surrounds you—this car on the tube." He was being funny as he was trying to freak me out, but he was right. Our decisions, actions, good and bad, successes and failures, all accumulate, all affect us, all impact how we act and react to whatever comes our way.

The question is, are we learning from the past? And are we courageous enough to heed those lessons and step bravely into the future?

When God Calls, Courage Answers

Courage that risks crossing into uncharted territories even as it holds fast to unwavering principles is a quality we see cropping up again and again in biblical leadership stories. God was asking men and women to be willing to step out and take risks that were impossible except for His help long before Walt Disney put his first animated drawing to paper.

Consider the story of Esther, a Jewish girl who just so "happens" to be in the right place at the right time in order to become part of a royal harem in Persia at the exact time when her people are facing genocide. Esther could've easily come up with some good reasons to do nothing—to take it easy and to play it safe.

When her cousin Mordecai did the unthinkable and asked her to go before the king on behalf of the Jews, she was afraid. It was punishable by death to address the king without first being spoken to. Not even being queen would save her. If the king was angered by her breach of protocol, then her death would have been swift.

But Mordecai said something that every Christian leader needs to hear: "And who knows but that you have come to your royal position for such a time as this?" (Esther 4:14). When Esther heard this—she did something that too few leaders are willing to do... she chose courage over personal comfort, and she embraced her purpose and didn't prioritize her safety.

As Christian leaders we must see that our leadership is about something greater than ourselves. Esther made a choice, and it changed the course of history. She actually said, "If I perish, I perish" (verse 16). She was choosing to sacrifice it all, if necessary, for something more important than herself.

In his own way (and not in as dire of circumstances such as potential genocide, or even personal peril) that's the level of courage that Walt Disney exhibited when he made Snow White. It was not carelessness; it was purposeful, and deliberate. Walt had worked for years refining his craft, building an organization, developing as a storyteller, and crafting his reputation in the entertainment world. He could have played it safe, protected his reputation, and preserved his financial success. However, when it came time to take a big risk to accomplish the next step toward his vision, he was ready and he was willing.

The Anatomy of Godly Courage

Biblical courage is not the lack of fear, but it is taking action despite those feelings. God didn't tell Joshua, as the Israelites were poised to take the Promised Land, not to be afraid. What God did say was "Be strong and courageous" three times in the first chapter of Joshua. Why the repetition? God understood how courage is not simply a single decision; it's a choice we have to make each day.

Walt Disney had to make the decision to be courageous over and over again throughout the production of Snow White. All along the way, there were plenty of places where some suggested that the work could be watered down, corners cut, or to accept that good was good enough. Truly, the financial pressure was enormous. The technical challenges seemed insurmountable. The criticism was relentless.

But Walt had learned something that all Christian leaders must also come to see: great things don't happen without great courage, and great courage is fueled by a deep sense of purpose. Walt wasn't just making a movie; he was creating a new medium. He wasn't simply entertaining the masses; he was showing that animation had the potential to touch the human heart.

This reminds me of another biblical hero who figured out the relationship between purpose and courage. When the angel Gabriel visited Mary at her home to inform her that she would be giving birth to a baby who would be the Messiah, for all we know, Mary could have said no or listed the 101 reasons why she could not and would not possibly do what Gabriel said she would do. After all, it was going to be very inconvenient, culturally unacceptable, and it would change her future. But, instead of giving into the instant fear she must have felt, she said, "I am the Lord's servant. May your word to me be fulfilled" (Luke 1:38).

The act of courage that Mary demonstrated, was not because God had laid out a timeline, and shared with her the entire story that was going to unfold. No. She didn't possess the plan—but she had faith in the Planner. She had faith that her purpose had been revealed for "such a time as this."

The Risk That Changed Everything

When Snow White and the Seven Dwarfs debuted at the Carthay Circle Theatre, in December 1937, it was a magical night. At first, everyone in the theater seemed to be unsure of what they were about to experience. Then there was laughter at the right time. Gasps came where gasps were appropriate. Men and women even cried when Snow White appeared to die after eating the poisoned apple (sorry, should have said "spoiler alert"). Then when it ended the audience, which was made of many Hollywood movie moguls and movers and shakers, erupted into thunderous applause.

Walt realized he had something very special on his hands. It wasn't mere entertainment he created; it was an emotional trip beyond the medium. The risk had paid off; in ways he never could've imagined.

But what fascinates me about that night is that Walt's delight wasn't in the fact that a hit meant money (Snow White became the highest grossing film in its time). His satisfaction was purposeful. He had demonstrated to the world, including all the doubters and critics, that animation could be used to tell stories with depth, that quality would find its audience, and pursuing excellence by taking educated risks was worth the pain.

This is another point that every Christian leader must understand: The courage of risk-taking isn't about the excitement or an adrenaline rush, and it certainly isn't a competition to see who's the bravest. It's about stewardship. When God gives us talents, or opportunities, or resources—we are expected to do the most we can and do the best we can. We aren't supposed to play it safe and bury them in the ground.

Jesus told a parable about three servants who were each given different amounts of money (called talents) to invest. Two of them took risks, made investments, and doubled their master's money. One played it safe, buried his talent in the ground, and gave right back what he had been given. The master's response? He commended the two who took risks and condemned the one who played it safe (Matthew 25:14-30).

The point of the story is simple: God's not going to reward safe mediocrity. He is looking for dividends from the faith-filled use of all He's given us to use for His service.

Innovation Requires Insurrection

Walt Disney's courage in trying something new didn't stop with Snow White, in fact it seems to have inspired him to be even more daring. He followed that up with Pinocchio, a film which was in many ways a more advanced project, and which pushed the boundaries of animation even further. And then there was Fantasia, an ambitious fusion of classical music and animation of a magnitude never before seen.

Unfortunately, both films initially lost money. Adolf Hitler would not permit Pinocchio to be screened in Nazi Germany and Benito Mussolini disallowed it in Italy. With the European market shrinking—the financial impact was profound. Also, critics didn't get Fantasia, and show-goers weren't prepared for such an artistic approach to animation (much less: classical music wasn't everyone's cup of tea). But Walt wasn't discouraged. He knew something many leaders today don't: innovation frequently demands insurrection against the status quo.

It reminds me of the biblical story of Daniel living in Babylon. In the book of Daniel, King Nebuchadnezzar commanded everyone to worship his golden image. Daniel could have easily gone with the crowd and blended in. But that would have meant he went against his faith in God. He could have negotiated with the Babylonian authorities to determine how little he would have to do to keep himself safe and ensure that he wouldn't lose his cushy life in the palace. OR he could decide that he wouldn't be that person.

Even though he didn't know what was to come, Daniel was not afraid. After the dedication of the golden image, when the time came to worship it, Scripture says, "Daniel went home to his upstairs room where the windows opened toward Jerusalem. Three times a day he got down on his knees and prayed, giving thanks to his God, just as he had done before" (Daniel 6:10).

Notice that Daniel didn't flaunt his rebellion. He did not hold a street march or launch a public relations campaign. He didn't rush to social media and scream into the echo chamber of his followers, trying to create the illusion that everyone agreed with him. And he didn't make sure that everyone could see him being faithful just so they would say, "Look at that Daniel being so faithful, isn't he amazing." Instead, he just quietly did the right thing, regardless of the cost that might come.

In his own way, Walt Disney led with this silent kind of courage all throughout his life. While everybody was telling him animation is not art, he just ignored them and quietly continued upping his game. When detractors announced that television would ruin the movies, he responded quietly by showing his support for the new medium and launching The Wonderful World of Disney. While everyone was saying that theme parks were not dignified, dirty, often sketchy, and even outdated forms of family entertainment, Walt didn't argue or fight. He just quietly kept designing Disneyland.

The Courage to Start Over

Nowhere was Walt's courage more visible than in his willingness to call a do-over when things weren't working. When his first animation company failed, he viewed it as an education. He learned from it and started Disney Brothers Studio.

When the movie industry was transformed with the addition of sound and critics were crying about it being just a fad (a nice lie they were telling themselves so they could attempt to maintain the status quo), Walt didn't worry over learning something new, nor was he resistant to the change. He accepted the challenge and introduced Mickey Mouse in Steamboat Willie with synchronized sound.

It really does take a different level of courage to be willing to start over, to reinvent yourself, or to know you must learn something new. It is hard to admit that what you're doing isn't serving you or your mission or your team, and then mustering the strength to start over if necessary. Most of us would simply rather keep doing the same thing we've always done, even if whatever it is isn't working any longer. And let's be honest, more times than we are comfortable admitting, we have all tried to stick our head in the sand and ignore the changing world around us.

I have found myself on many occasions arguing a point that I knew was probably wrong, outdated, or irrelevant— just because if I could keep it in play—I could keep doing what I have always done. Unfortunately, that doesn't work for long. I have always styled myself as a lifelong learner, and growth is one of my top five values, but having the courage to let go of what I know to learn something new or grow in a different direction is always challenging.

In the New Testament, we find an excellent example of adaptive courage in the Apostle Paul. This man was a merciless persecutor of Christians, but he was open to evolving—to having his eyes opened to new ideas (even the unwelcome idea that he might have been wrong). Remember—while his experience was dramatic—he could have chosen the darkness over the blinding light. However, when he said, "yes", and the punisher was turned into the proclaimer he didn't ease his way into it, didn't phase it in slowly, incrementally step by step, little by little. No, Paul realized he was in the wrong—and he changed.

Walt Disney was nothing if not flexible and adaptable. He embraced the vast sea of emerging technology. He pivoted when it had to happen, in small ways and seismic ways. And he had the knack for shapeshifting to remain relevant to society. But he was never willing to compromise on quality. He never forgot his values and his vision—so he always stayed focused on bringing people joy and magic.

The Cost of Courage

Walt understood something every Christian leader must understand. The price of courage is always better than the price for cowardice. Short-term safety is cozy but leads to regret in the long-term. If we don't have the courage to act, grow, and change when we know we should, we shouldn't be surprised when doors close and with them potential.

What would the world look like if Walt had given up after his first company went under? We never would have met Mickey Mouse. Snow White wouldn't have been created. We wouldn't have had Disneyland. None of the other myriad characters, movies, and theme parks would have been dreamed up. And, more significant, every family that has ever been touched by the magic of Disney's entertainment over those years would have missed out on that happiness and magic.

Biblical leaders as well: What if Moses thought it too dangerous to confront Pharaoh? Israel would have remained in bondage. What if David didn't fight Goliath because he was afraid of losing? Israel could have bowed under the oppression of the Philistines. What if the disciples failed to preach the Gospel after the ascension due to fear of persecution? There would have never been a Christianity beyond Jerusalem.

Courage will cost, but cowardice always costs more—it costs us our purpose, our potential, and our influence.

Building Courageous Organizations

One of Walt's greatest skills in leadership was that he created a culture that not only encouraged courage it rewarded it. He challenged his crew to take chances, break the rules, learn, and innovate in the pursuit of excellence even when it seemed unachievable.

To build this culture, Walt didn't just hire people who could do the job; he hired optimists who believed in his vision and were willing to go through hell and high water to achieve it. He assembled people who were on fire with excitement about the concept of building something the world had never seen.

Walt also set up the systems that allowed that to happen, that encouraged people to take those kinds of risks. He founded Disney University to train students with both technical skills and company culture. He also advocated for a culture of experiment and innovation, in a safe space. Not every idea would be a success, Walt understood, but each new trial was a valuable lesson.

Most importantly, Walt epitomized the sort of behavior he demanded from his employees. If his crew saw Walt taking risks, spending his own money, and keeping on when he made mistakes, then they were prepared to do the same.

This was not unlike how Jesus created His team. He did not go after the best talents in society; instead, He called those who were willing to leave all behind for His sake. He poured Himself into teaching them and training them. Ultimately, He taught them the power of courage and sacrifice when they saw Him die on the cross.

Today's Christian leaders have a similar opportunity. The institutions and organizations we create should be places of courageous participation, where new ideas are continually rewarded and where money is spent in service of trying to do something worthwhile. Also, we should hire the people who share our values and resonate with our callings, vision, and cause—not simply the ones that check the boxes in terms of technical skills.

The Fear Factor

So, let me tackle the elephant in the room: fear. Every leader must deal with fear, and there are times when that fear is justified. Walt Disney had many good reasons to be fearful. To start with, the animation industry was unproven. Second, technology either kept advancing rapidly or lagging behind. Third, the competition. There was no end to people who literally wanted to put Walt Disney out of business. And fourth, the money. He survived so much of the time on a shoestring budget. But after miles and miles of Disney films, more than 200 original enterprises and companies, I don't believe Walt Disney let any of those fears control him. Instead, Walt discovered how to control his fear rather than letting it control him. He always had good people around him and he was very willing to learn.

We can see this in the biblical story at multiple points. When God told Gideon to command Israel's army against the Midianites, Gideon was paralyzed with fear. When God called Jeremiah as a prophet, Jeremiah was scared to death and said that he was too young. When, through the burning bush, God told Moses to challenge Pharaoh, he responded that he didn't speak well or know what to say.

God didn't miraculously take away their fears. But He was with them and provided them with everything that they needed to serve Him. He provided Gideon with a plan and then pared down his forces so that it came down to God, Gideon, and 300 men—and they won. To Jeremiah, He gave the ability to speak. He granted Moses the partnership of his brother, Aaron. Aaron would help carry the message and Moses wouldn't have to do the task alone. (Though I wonder if, after the whole "Golden Calf" thing, Moses regretted not just sucking it up and doing it all himself.)

God never promises to eliminate our fears. He promises, however, that He will be with us, and will give us power to encounter whatever frightens us.

Courage as Contagious

Another wonderful thing about courage is that it's contagious. When someone sees another person demonstrate authentic courage—not hubris, but carefully considered bravery grounded in ethics—that example encourages them to take equally courageous action themselves.

Like Walt Disney's daring to take a bold step to do more—to do "new"—that empowered his animators to even work without pay during the hard financial times of the studio. They saw his courage, and they believed in his vision, so they took the leap of faith with him. His "all in" courage and vision also encouraged investors to finance projects that in other circumstances would have seemed much too risky. They trusted Walt's vision and judgment. And, of course, his courage, vision, and passion excited people to embrace new forms of entertainment, new ideas in storytelling, and even new vacation destinations.

The same is true in biblical leadership. When the Israelites saw David's courage against Goliath, they were suddenly ready to get in on the fight. When the first Christians witnessed the apostles' and other early church leaders' courage in martyrdom, they became bold to spread the message. And the influence of a courageous example is still powerful in Christian leadership today. When my team sees me facing adverse challenges with integrity rather than expedience or when they see me taking values-based risks in ministry endeavors, then, whether I win or lose, succeed or fail, they know that they can take risks for the good of the vision.

The Innovation Imperative

Walt Disney was always innovating in every aspect of his business, and that required a significant amount of courage. He was never satisfied to just practice "vigorous inertia"—where you work very hard to stay right where you are. Walt knew that in a swiftly changing world, to stand still (or even attempt to do so) was actually to fall behind. Having the courage to constantly innovate became a core part of the Disney culture.

In a practical way, what that meant was that what they celebrated today as a triumph might be thrown on the trash heap tomorrow and replaced by something better. You always have to have the courage to stop doing something that's successful because there might be a better idea. Walt could have continued making Mickey cartoons forever—they were a hit and very profitable. Instead, he was prepared to say goodbye to past success in order to hope for the future.

When Snow White was a hit, he didn't simply make seven sequels. He made it a launching pad to his most ambitious projects yet. When Disneyland succeeded, he didn't simply construct new parks in different cities. He was already dreaming of EPCOT—an entirely different kind of place, one that would expand the boundaries of what a theme park could be. (His idea was to build what would be called "Walt Disney World" as the means to fund the construction of EPCOT.)

This willingness to innovate is deeply biblical. Yes, Jesus often quoted and echoed the prophets from the Old Testament, but He also announced a New Covenant. Yes, Paul would often go first to the synagogues in the community, but he also took the message of the Gospel to the Gentiles. Yes, the early church did carry over many ideas, symbols, and adapted practices from Judaism, but they also were the people who turned the world upside down with the message of Jesus Christ.

It's the same for leaders today—both Christian and secular. What worked in our grandparents' time isn't necessarily the answer today. We can't assume that what worked last year or last month or even just moments ago will work today or tomorrow. We must stay true to our values, our ethics, our vision, and our mission as we navigate risks and discover what's new.

Courageous Decision-Making

One of the most tangible dimensions of courageous leadership is decision-making. Walt Disney had to make tens of thousands of decisions during his life. Some of the choices were mundane, but many had very significant consequences. So, how did he pull the levers that continuously pushed the vision forward?

For one, Walt set clear standards which everyone could use as a baseline for judgment. Quality wasn't negotiable. Family-friendly content was a must. Innovation was expected. When he was forced to make some very difficult decisions, he would measure them against those enduring principles.

Second, Walt made it a priority to listen to trusted counselors but recognized that the ultimate decision was his. Walt knew that being a leader involved taking responsibility for results—whether things went right and wrong.

Last but not least, Walt was willing to actually take action before he had ALL the information. He couldn't wait until his data was perfect and he understood the full background, and he was confident about the outcome. Instead, Walt learned all he could, he consulted with experts in his field and others, and then he made a decision with the information he had at his disposal.

That is similar to the way wisdom operates in the Bible. When Solomon had the chance, he did not ask God for more information; he only asked to be wise in applying information. Nehemiah didn't wait for every conceivable obstacle to be cleared; instead, he crafted a plan based on what he knew and leaned heavily on God for the uncertainties.

This is the kind of courage that Christian leaders should show to the world. First, we should base our decisions on biblical principles. Second, we should ask for guidance from ethical advisers. Third, we should spend the time gathering what we need to know and not more (avoid getting trapped in "analysis paralysis"). Finally, we use the gifts God has placed in our care to advance the vision that God has placed in our heart. We act—even if the results are unclear.

The Courage to Persevere

While very few people talk about it, perseverance requires courage. After all, it is one thing to make a hard call, and another still to stick with it when things get tough. This unrelenting kind of courage is exactly what Walt Disney demonstrated throughout his career.

There were several moments while Snow White was in production when he probably could have argued in favor of calling it quits. The budget was going overboard. The technical challenges seemed insurmountable. The criticism was intense. But he pressed on with testing and trying and building toward his vision.

This was not obstinacy or pride: it was principle-inspired perseverance. Walt survived because he believed in the importance of his work: it mattered not just that he succeeded, but for the advancement of animation as an art form.

That same tenacity is a characteristic of leaders in the Bible. It was Job's profound confidence in God's goodness that enabled him to survive the kind of suffering no one could imagine. Paul was beaten, thrown into prison, and shipwrecked all because he knew with absolute certainty that he was called to be an apostle. The early Church continued because those who comprised it believed that the Gospel was the most valuable prize in all the earth.

Christian leaders today could do with a dose of this dogged, persistent courage. We are going to experience setbacks and naysayers and impediments. There will be times when it feels like a smart decision to quit. Yet, if we are convinced that God has called us to our present role and that our vision is one worth fulfilling, then we must be made of sterner stuff.

Faith in Action: Personal Application

What about us? What does it mean to walk in courage, and leave behind the hesitancy that plagues us most of the time? Is there a way to live with an eye toward the Kingdom?

First, **we must identify our calling and core values**. It's easier to find some courage when you know what is at stake! Walt believed in quality family entertainment, and that's what gave him the audacity to do everything he did. Our bravery must be based on our knowledge of what God has called us to do and to be, and the values we know please Him.

So... ask yourself:

1. What are my core values?
2. What is God calling me to do? To be?
3. What are the ideas or ideals I must never give up?

When we know these answers—the courage to lead really comes much easier because it's not about us.

Second, **the small courageous steps you take today will prepare you for the larger steps God may call you for tomorrow.** Walt Disney was able to build up his capacity and courage through taking one step at a time—little by little—decision by decision. To do a lot of small, more manageable risks... step by step—decision by decision. For you, it might look like speaking up in meetings when you've never done it before. Perhaps you suggest a new idea even if it may be shot down. Perhaps it's time to tackle a project that would stretch your skill set. And remember: Every small act of courage you practice reinforces and amplifies your capacity for the next act of greater courage.

So... ask yourself:

1. What are the small steps I need to take today—even if there is some risk?
2. What do I feel God is preparing me to do next?

Third, **since courage isn't about just being reckless, how can you prepare, learn, grow, develop, stretch, expand, etc.?** Walt Disney worked for years developing his skills and talents, building his teams, and studying his audience. The more you're prepared—grounded in your calling, values, and vision—the more confidence and assuredness you'll have to take the next leap when opportunity comes knocking.

So... ask yourself:

1. Where are the areas of your life that you need to grow, learn, prepare, stretch, etc.?
2. When you picture your vision—and you leading that vision—what skills do you need to lead that more powerfully?

Finally, **you were never supposed to do this alone.** Of course, God is with you. And you also need to cultivate a support system. You would absolutely benefit from mentors, advisors, peers, and coaches who can guide you, support you and hold you accountable. Cultivate relationships with people who will tell you the truth even when you don't want to hear it.

Walt Disney had people he could trust and who understood his vision and long-term goals. He had partners like his brother Roy, who handled the business side of things so Walt could concentrate on dreaming up the creative side.

So... ask yourself:

1. Who are in my inner circle?
2. Who can I turn to, ask questions of, be real with so that God can speak to me through them?

Faith in Action: Leadership Application

So, what does brave leadership really look like in action within your company or team?

Have you created or developed a culture that rewards thoughtful risk-taking? If you want people to be courageous, it needs to feel safe to fail while attempting something big. Walt Disney created a culture of experimentation—where failure was viewed as a means to grow.

If the failure was because of being unprepared or a failure of character, deal with that appropriately and move on. If the reason for failure was trying to do something complex, learn from it and go on. Share stories about when taking risks does pay off, applaud the people who take on difficult projects even if they don't reach their goals.

Hire for courage and character, not just competence. The reality is that many or most technical skills can be trained, but it is significantly harder (or impossible) to train for courage and character. Walt Disney surrounded himself with people who shared his passion for excellence and, in turn, worked tirelessly to make it happen.

As you are hiring, always ask your candidates to share examples of when they've taken risks or worked their way through a difficult situation while holding on to their principles. Look for examples in their past where they have demonstrated character traits similar to yours and your culture. Don't make character a tiebreaker; instead, put it as an overall priority.

Model courageous leadership personally. I cannot overcommunicate this—your team is watching you all the time. They're also watching to see how you respond to pressure, make hard calls, and shift gears when things aren't going according to plan. If you want your team to be courageous, you must show them courage. That means being "open and transparent" about the kinds of challenges your organization is facing, sharing your thinking with people so they can understand how you're processing things in terms of risk and opportunity, and being quick to admit when you screwed up and what you learned from it. Own your decisions and the consequences that come with them, don't make excuses or point fingers when the wheels fall off.

Further, **invest in developing the courage of others.** Courage is a trainable skill, and humans can be coached and supported in developing their own. Walt Disney created Disney University, in part, to foster the courage of his people to lead and try new things. For you, this translates into creating a culture of learning. Spend time and money for you and your team to go to conferences, to read books together, and to invest in other professional development opportunities that challenge you and your team and helps build courage.

The Courage Legacy

Walt Disney's legacy is not only in the entertainment empire he created but also in the courage he exemplified and inspired others to have. His readiness to take chances, experiment incessantly, and to endure countless professional failures and personal losses helped create cultural values that continue to exist in the company long after his death. And, next to that, stands Walt's life as a powerful testament: ordinary people can do extraordinary things so long as they are courageous enough to stick with their vision.

Walt was a farm boy from Missouri, who learned how to draw, work hard, and have the audacity to want more than that. As Christian leaders, who are followers of Jesus Christ, our courage is based on something greater: our trust in the God who calls us to share with Him in His Kingdom work. We don't have to lean on our strength, wisdom, or what we can produce, but on His great power and trust in His perfect timing.

It's not a matter of whether we will encounter moments at work or in life when we need courage—because we most certainly will. The question will be how we respond. Will we have faith or will we be fearful? Will we take risks so that God will help us see what He has put into place, or do we play it safe?

Walt Disney's personal journey is a testament to the fact that courage in pursuit of excellence, innovation and service yield greatness that will echo beyond our time. As Christian leaders we can do something even more remarkable: we can make an eternal impact that outlives death and follows us into life everlasting.

So how do you have the courage to color outside the lines? Not only in a creative or innovative ways, but as you stay faithful to the calling God placed on your life when He knit you together in your mother's womb. We will look at strategies in the next chapter.

For now, consider this: What are you doing in your life right now that takes more courage than you feel? Chances are, that's where the Lord wants to work. He doesn't call the equipped, He equips the called. Do not worry if He's given you a vision or a task that you just aren't yet courageous enough to carry out. He'll lend you all the courage you need to make that first step.

CHAPTER FOUR

When the Going Gets Tough, the Tough Keep Drawing

Perseverance and Resilience

With the successes of Steamboat Willie, Snow White, and so many cartoon shorts, you would think that everything was sunshine and roses at the Disney Studios. However, in 1941, things took an unexpected turn. At that point you could probably find Walt Disney sitting in his office at the studio looking at a stack of bills and wondering where on earth he'd find the money to pay them. His most recent films, Pinocchio and Fantasia, are artistic triumphs but were initially financial failures. World War II had shut down European markets, and Walt saw a large chunk of his income disappear.

Then came something that hit Walt even harder because it hit him in the heart—not just the wallet. There was an animator's strike. The Screen Cartoonist Guild (SCG) wanted to represent the animators at Disney Studios, but Walt worried that it would damage the culture he had built. The issues the SCG focused on were usual in most workplaces—there was a pay gap between the top animators and the lower-level staff. They also created a sense of panic related to the financial losses of Pinocchio and Fantasia, making the animators feel their jobs were in danger.

In May 1941, around half of the studio's workers walked out and went on strike for five weeks. This was a great division in Disney's family of artists. Some of Walt's most talented animators led the strike while others were loyal to him. While the strike was eventually settled through the help of federal mediation between the representatives of the SCG and Roy (Walt's brother), the emotional cost was enormous—Walt felt deeply betrayed by people he had thought were his friends. The atmosphere changed in the studio and many of those relationships were never recovered. The SCG representatives had painted Walt in very negative colors, and after the excitement of the strike was over, and the workers realized that Walt was still Walt and they had endorsed an image of him that wasn't true—their feelings of guilt made it hard to go back to "business as usual." Many soon expressed that they were part of ruining something that was very special.

To add insult to injury, in 1941, the bank decided to give Walt advice that he should stick to less expensive and less complicated projects. They told him that they loved the little mouse, so Walt should just stick to mouse movies. With movies like Fantasia, Walt was being more artistic than they wanted him to be. So, the bankers wanted him to play it safe and stop all the innovation. Even some of his closest advisers were beginning to suggest that it might be time for Walt to trim back his ambitions and concede that animation had its limits.

But Walt Disney did something that distinguishes great leaders from good ones: he persevered. Not because he felt like it—trust me, I am sure there were days when he didn't feel like it. Not because success was certain—it wasn't. Walt persevered because he understood—like all Christian leaders must understand—even (or especially) in those times when we don't feel up to it—the vision, the calling, the mission is too important to quit, or slow down, or back up. Perseverance is not based on how we feel, it is based on our conviction.

I know what some of you are thinking at this moment. "That's an easy thing to say if you're talking about some-body else's hardship." And you're right. We can see the need for courage from afar—it's living it up close that presents the real challenge. And I've been there. Some days, giving up doesn't feel simply okay but eminently sane. Especially, on those days when you've given all you've got and gotten nothing or nowhere. When those you have trusted have let you down. When you temporarily wonder if the vision that once drove you is really worth the effort. I want you to know I've thought about giving up, quit-ting, throwing in the towel, joining the circus, or selling ice cream.

But what I've learned over a few decades of leadership (and yes, I know that's amazing to think about because I DO still look so young) is that the leaders who make a difference in the long run are usually not necessarily the most talented or luckiest or even best funded. They're the people who keep going when they want to quit.

The School of Hard Knocks and Harder Lessons

1941 was not Walt Disney's first crisis, nor would it be his last. But it certainly was his seminal crisis. He heard all the critics telling him to lower his bar, dumb down his vision, and accept mediocrity as the price of stability. But he made a choice that would shape the rest of his professional life. He vowed that he would maintain his standards of excellence and stay true to his vision.

This decision resulted in one of the most unique chapters in Disney history: a goodwill tour of South America paid for by the US State Department. While he was there, Walt was researching the Latin American culture, and the result was two Disney classics: Saludos Amigos and The Three Caballeros. Those two films helped keep the company solvent during World War II but also reignited his interest in exploring the roots of good stories.

The Bible includes plenty of stories about perseverance and resilience, but, of course, there's the one that comes to mind first: Job. He experienced a complete loss—his possessions, his health, his children, and his good name. His friends said he must have done something wrong. His wife told him to "curse God and die." He even wondered if God had forgotten him.

But Job made one defining choice—an act of resilient faith. In Job 13:15, he said, "Though he slay me, yet will I hope in him." Job didn't understand why he was suffering. He saw nothing good that could come of his pain. But still he relied on God's character even when God's actions appeared confusing. That's the perseverance and resilience that transforms leaders and rewrites history. It's not about having all the answers or knowing exactly how things are going to shake out. It means deciding that your faithfulness to God's calling on your life is more important than whatever you are dealing with right now.

The Endurance Test

You know what I find interesting about Walt Disney and biblical leaders? Their greatest successes often seem to come after their worst season. So much of Walt's creativity and innovations of the 1940s-1950s were spawned by the 1941 financial and staff crises. At the end of his story, Job's restoration outweighed his loss. It seems to happen often enough that it's not an accident, but a trend. What this says to me is that God can use the toughest seasons we experience to prepare us for our most impactful season. The question is, will we hang on long enough to see the breakthrough?

Let's go back to the Old Testament and the story of Joseph. Joseph was a living illustration of this principle. Joseph was sold into slavery, falsely accused of ethical failings, and was ultimately forgotten in prison. I don't suppose any of us would have been astounded if he had grown cynical and lost hope (I'm not saying we would become cynical—well, yeah, I am.). Joseph was an honest man who was steadfast in his integrity, and he trusted and believed that "all things work together for good to them that love God."

So, when Pharaoh brought Joseph to the palace to interpret his dream, Joseph was ready. Through his connection to God, he was able to interpret the dream, and he had the courage to share the unfiltered story. There would be feast years and famine years. All of Joseph's personal "famine" years had conditioned him—the hard roads he had traveled had tempered him. So, he found his place in the Egyptian government overseeing their response to the dream. Joseph's trials had taught him things that triumphs could never do, and he was ready to step up in leadership.

Walt Disney had a similar type of lean years. The pressures of money taught him to be more strategic about allocating resources. From the strike, Walt had learned the value of clear communication and deliberate and unmistakable fair treatment for employees. The war years also taught him to be flexible and inventive in pursuit of new markets—and opportunities.

When the 1950s rolled around, Walt was planning Disneyland. In that process he drew on all the lessons he learned in good times and the bad. He structured the financing of the park more thoughtfully than he had the financing of his films. He invented better ways to manage groups of professionals. The tests hadn't defeated him—they had taught him.

The Nehemiah Strategy

Now, let's go back to Nehemiah and his leadership in restoring Jerusalem's walls. When Nehemiah had first seen the wreck, it seemed impossible. The walls had been in ruins for many years. The people were dispirited and scattered. The enemies surrounded the city, and, of course, they were against the rebuilding project.

Nehemiah understood this vital truth about perseverance: perseverance is not getting back out onto the field with enough strength to play that entire game from the whistle. It's about having enough strength to take the next right step, and then the next one, and then another.

So, Nehemiah persevered. He divided the task into relatively small sections for every family to do the work next to their own houses. When their enemies threatened to attack, he did not suspend the work—instead he armed the workers and put them on watch. And when people whined about the load, he didn't lower the bar—he heard their complaints and restructured the workflow.

The most important thing that Nehemiah did was that he kept his eye on the why of work. It wasn't just a matter of building a wall; the goal was to once again make Jerusalem a safe place for God's people to worship and serve Him. And when people focused on the purpose, more than the process, they found strength to continue.

Walt Disney did something like this as he was constructing Disneyland. The project was somewhat plagued by ongoing issues: rising costs, construction delays, skeptical investors, technological challenges, and so many other issues that had never been solved. Walt very well could have been intimidated by how grand the whole project was—there seemed to be enemies all over the place.

Instead, he approached it in bite-sized chunks. Disneyland was divided into Main Street and a series of lands (Fantasyland, Tomorrowland, etc.). Walt set a team to focus on each of the locations, a timeline specific to the issues of that area, and a plan to address any new issues that would arise. Every subplan fed into the general grand plan that would create a place where families could experience joy and magic.

As opening day grew near it became apparent that everything wouldn't be done. Walt made a decisive move: they would open what was ready and finish the rest according to its timeline. Perfection wasn't the enemy of progress, paralysis was. So, Walt didn't allow paralysis to stop his vision from going forward.

The Power of Process Over Feelings

Walt Disney and biblical leaders understood something that many modern-day leaders seem to miss—perseverance is a process. You persist not because you feel like it—you persist because you're devoted to the mission, the vision, the goal.

Throughout the years, Walt developed daily habits that helped him stay focused and grounded in the hard seasons. He would arrive at the studio early in the morning, walk around to see who was doing what work in various departments and then review storyboards and animation sequences before sitting down to think about long-term projects. These practices were a point of order and routine in an otherwise disordered environment.

In the Bible we are called to "walk by faith, not by sight" (2 Corinthians 5:7). That means choosing to develop faith habits so that we live a life according to God's promises and our calling—not feelings or circumstances. Consider the perseverance of the Apostle Paul who shook off years of relentless opposition, imprisonment, and hardship. He practiced spiritual disciplines—prayer, meditation on Scripture, fellowship with other believers—that anchored him regardless of his external circumstances. He also possessed a deep focus on life outside his own circumstances. Even in prison, Paul wrote some of his most encouraging letters. Stop and think about that for a second. He penned some of his most encouraging and powerful letters when he was the most oppressed.

This is the paradox of persistence and endurance: so many times, our greatest influence will not be in spite of our difficult times, but because of them. People are watching to see how we handle pressure and disappointment and setbacks. Truly, how we respond in such times, speaks more of us and our God than 1,000 sermons or testimonies about perseverance, resilience, courage, and faith.

The Innovation Born from Desperation

Something incredible happened to Walt Disney in times of his greatest adversity: he became more innovative, not less. The financial pressures he was under caused him to come up with some creative solutions to his issues. Technical limitations compelled him to develop new techniques.

The South American films he produced after his 1941 tour had kept the studio afloat during the war, and these films also brought fresh styles of animation and cultural motifs that would further open out Disney's storytelling techniques. Reduced cashflow required Walt and his team to be more efficient to produce better quality films for less money. The experience of attempting to compete with live-action movies compelled Walt to pioneer revolutionary advances in animation, which helped him in the journey toward Disneyland.

You will see this theme in the Bible and the history of faith as well. The persecution of early Christians didn't stop the spread of Christianity—it accelerated it. Because believers were dispersed beyond Jerusalem, the Gospel reached new regions. Paul's letters that were written while he was in prison would become much of the New Testament. The Apostle John was banished to the island of Patmos when he received the Revelation that would serve as the final book of the New Testament.

God appears to have this amazing ability of turning our weaknesses, our limitations, and even our circumstances into fuel for our creativity. If we don't take the easy way of doing things, perhaps we'll need to find better ways. When we don't have the usual tools or the typical circumstances, we have to get creative, we must develop new tools, new skills, new abilities that we have never known we were capable of.

That is a concept Christian leaders need to embrace today. Instead of seeing a challenge as an obstacle to our mission or a roadblock to our vision, it should always be seen as an invitation to innovation. Instead of talking about what we don't have—let's spend our time and energy imagining ways that we could do things to fulfill the vision with what we do have.

The Team That Perseveres Together

One of the reasons Walt Disney was able to persevere was that he didn't do it alone. He worked with people who shared his vision and his standards for quality. When the going got tough, they got tough together.

In 1941, Walt was devastated by the betrayal he felt from some of his animators who joined the strike. However, he gained critical insight into the construction of teams who can survive such turmoil. Shared hardship either binds people together or forces them apart. The trick is to have everyone understand not just what you're trying to do, but why it matters.

After the strike, Walt did a lot of soul searching on how he could improve his relationship with his employees. He initiated regular meetings to discuss the financials of the project they were working on, and to share what he was seeing in terms of long-term projects. He worked very hard to open channels of communication so that he could gather input and feedback. Most important, he made sure everyone knew they were part of something larger.

This gets me thinking about how Jesus trained His disciples to understand the importance of the mission to which they belonged. He didn't withhold the truth that it would be difficult to follow Him. He challenged other would-be disciples, and He didn't sugarcoat the cost. But, as an amazing leader, He sketched a picture of what their sacrifice would accomplish.

Jesus told His disciples that they would be persecuted, abused, mocked, and in the end, killed. But He also told them that they would be part of establishing God's kingdom here on earth, that their message would spread from one end of the earth to the other, and that what they built would not die with their sacrifice. Instead, their faithfulness to the vision would multiply over generations.

When the disciples began experiencing the things that Jesus had told them, they were not only intellectually prepared, but spiritually prepared. They understood that their pain was for a purpose, that their calling meant something, and that they were part of something bigger than themselves.

Christian leaders today must do likewise. We need to be honest with our teams about what we're facing and remind them of why we keep going, day in and day out. When they understand why their sacrifice is meaningful, people can endure the most extreme hardship imaginable.

The Compound Effect of Consistency

Walt Disney's perseverance was not the sort that you hear about in the big movie epics in the golden age of Hollywood. Every day, Walt simply kept working. He kept improving. And he kept believing in his vision even when there seemed to be very little forward movement or no progress at all. His perseverance was lived out in the daily decisions he made to stay focused on his vision, and because he made those decisions, he saw his dreams become reality.

Consider how Mickey Mouse evolved from an ordinary character in Steamboat Willie into a global sensation.

This didn't happen overnight. It was just one cartoon after another, each one slightly better than the last. Thousands and thousands of drawings, all better than the one before it. Countless hours of voice work and story development and character tweaking. (Walt himself was the voice of Mickey Mouse from 1928-1947.)

The same holds true for spiritual maturity and leadership growth. More often than not, we do not "grow up" spiritually through a sudden transformational experience (though God can obviously work in such a way if He chooses, but those experiences are often the first step in a journey). But by choosing, every single day, to do what's right, not what's easiest, safest, most familiar, or most convenient. When we do so, we become the kind of people and the kind of leaders we all respect—those who choose service over selfishness, and who choose to keep our eyes and hearts focused on others, no matter how great the personal cost.

In the Bible, you might find this as "being faithful with a few things," so that God will give us more to take care of (Luke 16:10). Every time you choose obedience when it would be simpler to give up; every time you stay when you want to run away; every time you're faithful when no one is looking—that's how character-based leaders are made. And when we do those things, we get more opportunities to do MORE of those things.

It's the sort of thing that Walt Disney seemed to naturally understand. Excellence is not a singular act; it is a habit. Quality is not a destination; it is a constant journey. And, it is not about just getting the one big win, it is about the series of small wins that keeps you moving toward fulfilling your vision.

The Refinement Process

This is something that biblical leaders learned, and Walt Disney did too: sometimes adversity tests us, but it also perfects us. The issues we face are not just something to overcome, but opportunities for us to grow to be the kind of person that can handle greater opportunities.

Walt's first business failure, for example, taught him so much about what he did wrong. Later, with the loss of Oswald the Lucky Rabbit, he learned about contract negotiation and the value of protecting intellectual property. His lessons on diversification and risk management came from the 1941 crisis. He had learned from each defeat, and it was the sum of these lessons that opened the door to success.

The Bible refers to it as refining: "But He knows the way that I take; when He has tried me, I shall come forth as gold" (Job 23:10). Gold is purged in the fire, not to consume it, but to make it purer and brighter. Just as any good mother or father doesn't shelter their child and protect them from every battle, God didn't create us to be protected away from hard times; He uses those struggles so that we grow into the person He knows we can be with the skills, aptitudes, and attitudes that give us the ability to make an ever greater impact.

This perspective can change our vision of hard times. Rather than asking, "Why me?" we can wonder, "What is it about this experience that God can help me learn?" It's a change in mindset that allows us to not obsess over what we are losing, but, rather, we look at what we could be gaining. This enables us to think of our setbacks differently—not as failing, but simply as practicing and learning for something else.

This is a perspective Walt Disney held his whole career. And when Pinocchio was a financial flop at first, he didn't abandon ambitious storytelling. Instead, he studied what was resonating with audiences and polished his style. When the war cut off his European markets, he didn't take refuge in purely domestic projects. He expanded into new markets and broke ground with new kinds of content.

For Walt, focusing on constant learning and improvement were some of his biggest strengths throughout his life. He continually questioned himself about what he could do better, what he could learn from his successes as well as his failures, and how every experience was preparation for the next.

The Long View

One of the reasons Walt Disney was such a great role model on perseverance is because of his perspective on life. When quarterly or annual results didn't measure up, he remained focused on the decades of impact he wanted to have.

It was this vision that allowed him to make very expensive decisions that looked unjustified in the short run but became a gold mine in the long-term. This was true for his early investments in breakthrough animation technologies like the multi-plane camera (which allowed animated shorts and feature films to show depth of scenery and characters) and the creation of Disneyland—both required enormous upfront investments and didn't start delivering profit for several years. This long-view was what enabled Walt to do something today even when the payoff wouldn't come until tomorrow (or ten years later).

The Bible repeatedly calls leaders to use this long-view lens. For example, Abraham was promised that his descendants would be as many as the stars in the sky, but he did not see that promise fulfilled in his lifetime. Moses led the Israelites from Egypt to the borders of the Promised Land but never entered it. David collected the supplies for the temple, but Solomon built it.

These leaders understood that they served an eternal God. A God whose timeline preceded them and would extend far beyond them. Their life, their service, their leadership was just part of a greater story that God was writing. They were called to do their part because what God was doing was bigger than them. If they were the leader that God called them to be, then, while they may not immediately see or ever experience the result, they would be part of something that would reach down through the generations.

This long-term view is precisely what Christian leaders need today. We are not just building our businesses, ministries, or families for ourselves. We are the stewards of today. And what we do has the possibility to transform lives, communities, and the future. This perspective is what makes you keep moving forward even when the present is hard or the short-term results are bad.

Perseverance with Purpose

Here is something that will likely offend you: Perseverance without purpose is only stubbornness. Walt Disney didn't win simply because he was too proud to lose. He kept going because he believed what he was trying to do was worth doing.

Walt's vision was to provide quality family entertainment that would bring joy and magic into people's lives. It wasn't a business mission statement; it was a personal belief system that spurred him to act, even when it cost him.

When Roy and the finance people pushed Walt to cut corners on quality and save money with Snow White and countless other projects, he said no because it would be a disservice to the families who trusted and depended on the quality of his product. When his distributors demanded that he make cheap cartoons for a fast buck, he said no because he knew that he could never stretch the medium of animation if he just did what he had always done.

This kind of perseverance is a theme throughout the Bible. Noah was ridiculed as he built the ark because he believed God's word that there would be a flood. Jeremiah prophesied under persecution because he believed everyone needed to hear God's message. Paul was willing to endure being in jail and being beaten because he believed the Gospel was worth suffering for no matter what.

In each case, each person was persistent because they believed that the destination was worth the journey, that the end was more important than comfort, convenience, or personal gain. When we know for whom we do what we do, and why our work is important—to us as well as to God and others—we can find the strength to press forward, even when the road gets tough. Not because we are stubborn and entrenched, but because we are visionary and faithful.

Building Resilient Systems

Walt Disney learned firsthand that perseverance is not just about human will power, it's the ability to create systems that can weather the storm. When Walt had survived the turmoil of 1941, he reorganized his company in a way to ensure it could withstand anything that came along the way in the future.

He diversified his revenue sources, creating income streams in a number of ways beyond the theatrical releases. He built up bigger financial reserves to cushion any unanticipated declines. He upgraded communications systems to prevent the kind of misunderstandings that helped drive the strike. He created more participatory processes by which he could make decisions and access the wisdom of his team.

These were not simply business enhancements; they were strategies for perseverance. Walt learned you can't survive solely on good intentions. He had to organize the organization so that it could sustain for the long haul.

The early Church operated on similar principles. They did not just rely on the personal charisma and dedication of the apostles. They created systems for leadership training, financial assistance, conflict management, and doctrinal purity. It was these structures that allowed Christianity to grow even as individual leaders were persecuted or dying.

Today's Christian leaders must do the same. We must build organizations that will outlive us. That includes growing other leaders, establishing clarity around processes and procedures, achieving financial security, and instilling cultures that preserve where we came from and where we are going even when we are no longer there.

The Testimony of Endurance

Here's something miraculous about perseverance: It can lead to a testimony that remains uplifting to others long after the challenge or event has passed. Long after a leader has left this world, people will still tell the story of their faithfulness and perseverance, their dedication to the vision and the cause, their willingness to sacrifice, and their servant leadership. OR they will tell a completely different story.

People are still inspired by the way Walt handled the crisis in 1941, how he supervised the construction of Disneyland, and how he maintained his commitment to quality when it was fiscally risky to do so. By effectively leading in these times and these ways, his story still encourages others to cast aside the limitations of their own obstacles, and to stay committed to their vision and their purpose. (You are reading this book!)

We are also inspired by the perseverance found in many of the stories in the Bible. The faith of Job in the midst of all his suffering has been an inspiration for millions across the millennia. Paul's absolute faithfulness when he was imprisoned has inspired and encouraged missionaries, pastors, and other Christians throughout the ages. The ability of the early Christians, who faced persecution after persecution, to keep going—to keep spreading the Gospel—to keep teaching the world through precept and example what it means to be a disciple—has inspired many others who are facing their own trials.

You are creating a testimony or witness through your faithfulness and perseverance. People are observing how you handle pressure, disappointment, and defeat. Your answers, attitudes, and actions are giving them a picture of the kind of person you are, of the principles to which you hold, and what manner of God you trust. Every time you persevere under it with a measure of grace, honor, and faith, you give others the inspiration and permission to do the same in their situation.

That's what Christian leadership is all about: not checking off lists and achieving quotas. We show what it means to take a stand for the glory of Christ on the playing field of life. Our steadfastness, our perseverance is a part of our own ministry, it's a part of our witness, and will be part of our legacy.

Faith in Action: Personal Application

So, how do we develop that kind of persistence/endurance/determination in our own leadership journey? How do we build the resilience to weather the storms that every leader experiences?

First, **clarify what you want to achieve beyond self-advancement**. The thing that kept Walt Disney driven was he wanted to create quality family entertainment. So, your persistence cannot just be for self-advancement or satisfaction.

Take some time to think about the higher purpose behind your work:

1. How does your leadership bless others?
2. What kind of legacy do you want to leave behind?
3. What can you do to further God's kingdom as part of your job?

Once you have the reason why you're persevering clear in your mind, you will have strength to keep going when the going is tough.

Second, **create daily habits that give you anchors when the stormy weather comes**. Both Walt Disney and the great leaders of the Bible lived by strong routines and habits so that their life was consistent and reliable regardless of what storm currently raged around them.

- Cultivate spiritual disciplines of prayer, Bible reading, and worship that will help you anchor your soul to God's strength and perspective.
- Cultivate personal habits such as disciplined planning, take time to "climb onto the balcony" to get the long-view of where you are going AND where you want to go.
- Cultivate personal habits and routines like physical exercise, getting adequate sleep, and maintaining healthy relationships to help sustain you even in challenging times.

Third, **construct systems that are conducive to long-term sustainability**. Your sheer force of will won't be enough; you also need organizational tools and systems that can make it through the trials of life.

- Create multiple streams of income (or legs) to financially support all you are doing or want to achieve.
- Establish reliable means of communication with your key people (family and friends), so that in the challenging times people are less stressed or worried.
- Set aside reserve funds for the unexpected.
- Surround yourself with like-minded individuals who can help share the load in difficult seasons.

Fourth, **take on a learning posture during rough times**. Rather than just trying to get through challenges, look for what it can teach you.

- Write in a journal about what difficult times have taught you.
- Find mentors that have struggled through similar challenges.
- Read biographies of people who have pushed through challenges.
- Think of setbacks as nothing less than education.

The more you understand and learn in painful seasons, the better you'll be equipped for what's to come.

Faith in Action: Leadership Application

How do you cultivate perseverance and resilience in your team or organization?

Build a culture that values persistence over instant wins. If you want your team to thrive and survive, celebrate the right behaviors. Walt Disney nurtured the culture of valuing good craftsmanship and audacious experimentation even when it took more time and resources than easier options.

Find and recognize the teammates who are determined to even do the hard projects right, who hold to the high-quality bar under pressure, who understand that failure is their opportunity to learn. Share stories about instances when perseverance led to a breakthrough. Create metrics that measure the results of the long-term, not just progress in the near term.

Share purpose regularly, particularly in challenging circumstances. People persevere when they have a sense that what they do makes a difference. Walt Disney became very transparent about the company's mission and why the resulting difficult decisions were being made.

In tough times, communicate more, not less. Describe not just what choices you're making, but why. Connect smaller tasks to larger goals every day. Help people see how their contributions contribute to the organization's mission.

Strengthen your organization to be more durable. Lose the one-man heroics as the way to face problems. Design systems that can create success and survive disruptions.

Crosstrain your team members so that work isn't held up when key people are out. Create formal decision-making structures that are not dependent on the availability of a single person. Create communication systems that function when disasters strike. Build up financial reserves to help you ride out unexpected storms.

Develop other pace setters who are able to endure and persevere. Your organization's long-term health depends on there being several people who can lead through tough times. Walt Disney invested in leadership development (creative and business) that would carry out the work of the company.

Pinpoint the up-and-coming stars and allow them the chance to grow as they help lead in good times and face the hard times. Share your process for making tough decisions so others will get the hang of being strategic in difficult times. Create mentor programs that pair seasoned team members with newer ones.

Practice patience with yourself. Your team needs to see that resilience is possible, but they also need to learn that it requires vulnerability. Walt Disney was candid about the struggles that the company faced—and he shared his commitment to dealing with them.

Be open about the times when you are confronted with challenges and difficulties, but don't allow those issues to lead you or your organization into negativity.

What do you find yourself hopeful and motivated about at this time?

Be open to admitting when you screw up or need to change directions. Show that persistence is not about being perfect; it's all about being doggedly committed to your vision and mission.

The Perseverance Promise

Walt Disney's story teaches us that while perseverance doesn't guarantee we get through everything the way we planned, it turns us into someone who can handle whatever comes next.

Throughout his career, Walt was hit with bankruptcy, battled the banks, went through strikes, was stabbed in the back by friends, and countless other challenges. Every obstacle shaped him, chiseled his character, and prepared him for the next breakthrough. By the time Disneyland opened in 1955, the man who had been bilked out of the rights to Oswald the Lucky Rabbit as a naïve young animator in 1928 was significantly stronger and smarter.

The same transformation is promised to us in the Bible as we go through trials and make it through them with faith: "Consider it pure joy, my brothers and sisters, whenever you face trials of many kinds, because you know that the testing of your faith produces perseverance. Let perseverance finish its work so that you may be mature and complete, not lacking anything" (James 1:2-4).

The point is not simply to suffer through a grueling season, but to emerge from this on the other side stronger and wiser and better equipped to give of oneself in service to God's work. Perseverance makes us not avoiders of struggle but conquerors of it and helps us not become those who flee challenges, but leaders determined to face them.

Walt Disney taught us that if we hold our course—if we are faithful to our vision—anything is possible. If we set a high bar and meet it, the result can last long after we are gone. As Christian leaders, we have an opportunity to offer something even better: character that incarnates into our world a reflection of God's own heart and an influence that expands His Kingdom.

It's not a matter of IF you will experience seasons where your perseverance and endurance is truly tested—you will. The question will be what you do with those seasons to equip yourself for life and leadership in a way that God can use ultimately in His best interests.

So, please remember this word of hope. The same God who supported and sustained all of the people of faith through ages past is the very same God who wants to support and sustain you as you face whatever it is that lies before you. The true question is, will you have the stamina/guts/determination to keep pressing on doing what you know is right, doing what you know brings Him glory, doing what you need to do to fulfill the vision He has given you?

God's timing is perfect, God has unlimited resources, and God only wants the best for you. It isn't your job to figure out or control every outcome. Your job is to be faithful to His calling and let Him take care of the results. It's that kind of perseverance/persistence/endurance that changes the world—one day, one choice, and one act of faithfulness at a time.

CHAPTER FIVE

Excellence Is Never an Accident

Excellence and Quality

Let's circle back and expand:

It was 6:45 p.m., Dec. 21, 1937, and Walt Disney was waiting anxiously in the lobby of the Carthay Circle Theatre in Hollywood. It was the night that Snow White and the Seven Dwarfs was premiering, and Walt was terrified. He didn't think the film was bad—after all, he had been obsessed with its production for three years—going over each frame of film, every song, and every aspect of its creation. He was fearful because, before too long, he would find out if his pursuit of perfection was worth what it cost him.

The film cost $1.5 million, a substantial sum for feature film made in 1937 (The Life of Emile Zola, the live action movie that won Best Picture that year, only cost $1.2 million.). Walt had asked his artists to employ techniques more advanced than any filmgoer had ever witnessed: lifelike animation of humans, elaborate multiplane camera sequences, and a full orchestra recording the soundtrack. Whenever his artists came to him with ideas about how they might skimp and therefore save money and time during production, Walt's message to the team was crystal clear. They weren't just making a cartoon, they were producing something that families all over the world were going to treasure for years to come. Therefore, no corners would be cut, and even the smallest detail was important.

When the movie started, while sitting with Lillian in the theater, Walt could hardly watch the screen. He spent most of the time watching the people. He had seen Snow White hundreds of times throughout the production, scrutinizing every frame and urging his team to reanimate scenes that were good but not great. This was the test: would his creation speak to people who had never seen anything like it before?

What he did that night changed the landscape of entertainment forever. He truly did create an animated full-length story that had audience members of all ages engaged. When the words, "The End," appeared on the screen, the crowd in the theater rose, clapping and cheering as the credits rolled. Even the critics declared it a masterpiece.

And here's what's amazing about that night: even though Walt Disney was surely happy about the financial success of the movie (Let's be honest… his finances were as tight as the lid on a pickle jar.), more than just the money, what was fulfilling for him was his insistence on high-quality had paid off and allowed him to offer up something worthy—a product that would last and continue to bring joy and magic into families for generations.

The Pursuit of Something Greater

You see, when you pursue excellence—that doesn't mean you are chasing perfection, or you are simply trying to "one-up" someone or something just for the sake of "one-upping." It's about stewardship. God wouldn't give us talents, opportunities, and resources unless there was an expectation that we would use them to their fullest. Excellence is our giving back our best to Him and by making the biggest difference we can possibly make.

This is something that Walt Disney never described in religious terminology but lived out intuitively. Simply put, he got it. He wanted to give audiences the best he had to offer. But this was not only good business sense—and it was certainly that—it was a moral principle underlying every decision he made.

This reminds me of a man who is described in Exodus 31—a craftsman named Bezalel (Yes, you can pause reading this book and go look him up. I didn't make up the name just to test your biblical knowledge.). When God commanded the people of Israel to construct a tabernacle for worship, God didn't just grab someone who was "good enough" for the job. He picked Bezalel, upon whom He "put the Spirit of God and filled with wisdom in understanding, in knowledge and in all kinds of skills" (Exodus 31:3).

God was precise in what He wanted the tabernacle to look like, and the level of quality to which He wanted it built because it would be a reminder of His presence with His people. The draperies, the carved wood, and the inset precious metals needed to do justice to what it symbolized. What was remarkable about Bezalel's talent was not merely that he had skill and craftsmanship but rather, his artistry was an act of worship.

Walt Disney shared a similar sort of reverential attitude toward his work. He understood that the joy he gave would be stitched into people's happy memories. A child's first introduction to one of his movies, shorts, or one of his many characters was potentially forming their ideas of what storytelling looked like and maybe giving them inspiration for life. A family visit to Disneyland had the possibility to create core memories and lifelong bonds. How could he not do his absolute best with that kind of responsibility?

The Anatomy of Excellence

Here's something I found after decades of studying leaders great and small: excellence is never an accident. It is always the result of true intention, earnest effort, intelligent direction, and skilled execution. It's the wise choice—among many options.

Walt Disney did not bumble his way to genius. He had a systematic way of thinking about the mechanics of great storytelling, he constantly put those learnings into action by hiring the best talent that he could find, and he was always looking for and willing to accept new ways to bring his vision to life through cutting-edge methods. Plus, he did all of this without ever sacrificing quality—even when it would have been more convenient and profitable.

Circle back to what we have said about Snow White. The characters in the cartoons that preceded his first full-length film were caricatures: exaggerated, simplified, and comical. But Walt wanted Snow White to be a human—someone the audience could relate to.

The process of getting there, while well thought out, was not easy at all. For all the human characters in the film, Walt employed live-action reference models. He thought about how fabric moved, how light fell on faces, how mood was conveyed in small tremors of posture and expression. He had his animators spend months studying all those things and more to be able to draw human anatomy with realistic accuracy.

When the animators' early attempts failed to meet Walt's standard, he didn't settle for what they had produced or announce that what he wanted had proved to be impossible. No, he decided to invest in his artists. He spent money training his animators, bringing in outsiders to teach advanced techniques and checking every scene himself to ensure that it supported his vision of the movie.

This quality carried over into all other areas as well. Walt was determined that there would be a full orchestra to play the score for the movie. This meant that he had to hire composers and arrangers to prepare music for an entire orchestra, and that was in addition to hiring an entire orchestra. He used some of his limited funds to invest in the development of the multiplane camera. By painting the background for each scene on different panels of glass, Walt could add movement and depth by shooting the scene though all of the glass plates at one time. Of course, that meant painting multiple glass plates for every scene—more time, more effort, more cost. Finally, Walt hired professional actors to perform the voices for the characters, rather than just using associates of his studio.

Each of those decisions was more expensive and took longer. But Walt knew that quality was an investment that yielded a return. The reward you get for investing enough to do something right the first time is truly greater than what you would have to pay across the years when you settle for mediocrity.

The Solomon Standard

This principle of stewardship appears to be a major theme throughout the Bible. When King Solomon built the Temple, he didn't just go to work with whatever gold or stone was at hand. He waited until he could create something perfect. He imported the cedars of Lebanon, the gold of Ophir, and artists from neighboring kingdoms. Why? Because the building that he was building would contain the glory of God.

First Kings 6:7 reads, "The temple, when it was built, was built of stone finished at the quarry, so that no hammer or chisel or any iron tool was heard in the temple when it was built." Just think about it. Every stone was cut to a specific size before being brought to the construction site. No shortcuts. No "close enough." No "we'll fix it later."

This was really more than just a show of beautiful artistry or merely a display of Solomon's wealth and power. That was done to demonstrate that God is worthy of our very best. God is worthy of our best thinking, our best preparation, and our best work. So, when we are representing our God in our world (and all of us do, if Christ is in you), then good enough isn't good enough, mediocre will never cut it, and less than our best is just disrespectful and ungrateful.

Walt Disney was a man who adhered to this rule as well, though his temple was constructed not from stone and gold but celluloid film and dreams. He knew the tales he spun, whether about villainous queens or lasting love—could trigger a child's imagination, affect life within the home, and ensure memories that would stick with people until their dying day. With that power, why would he ever skimp?

While in production on Fantasia, Walt realized the potential of combining classical music and animation. Walt expanded the project astronomically because he envisioned complex sequences that had never been done before. Just the "Sorcerer's Apprentice" scene required advances in animation, sound, and color technology.

When Walt's advisors proposed to scale down the project to save money, he refused. Like he said in describing Snow White: "There would be no compromise on money, talent or time."[5] He understood that the demonstration of animation-as-high-art required relentless, uncompromising commitment to nothing less than excellence—no matter how expensive it became.

---

[5] Walt Disney, speech accepting the Showman of the World Award from the National Association of Theatre Owners, October 1, 1966.

Excellence As Evangelism

Here's something amazing about excellence: it preaches without ever having to say a word. When people encounter something that is genuinely excellent, when they see a Disney movie or see some craftsmanship or experience an excellent organization—there's a powerful recognition that it was done right and it was done to its best. Sadly, because so many settle for mediocre in today's world, our interaction with excellent is a very special experience.

It was a lesson learned long ago by Walt Disney. In 1928, Steamboat Willie was not just another cartoon. Walt ensured that it had fluid animation, appealing character designs and personalities, and those things set it apart from its competition. But then Walt made it excellent by synchronizing everything with sound. Action and sound came together in seamless beauty.

Before Steamboat Willie, people already knew that a Disney Brothers cartoon was going to be made with quality and would be very entertaining. However, after the world met and heard Mickey Mouse as Steamboat Willie, the audience began to expect what they experienced in that groundbreaking moment—excellence.

Remember the story of the talents that is found in Matthew 25. In Jesus' story, the servants who put their master's money to work—investing it wisely and profitably—were not handsomely rewarded with an early retirement. No, because they were excellent stewards of what had been placed in their care, they were entrusted with more responsibility. "Well done, good and faithful servant!

You have been faithful with a few things; I will put you in charge of many things" (Matthew 25:21).

Excellence creates opportunities for excellence. Great work leads to great opportunities. Faithfulness over little things readies us for bigger things.

Go back to the Old Testament Story of Daniel. When Daniel was hauled away as a captive to live and serve in Babylon, he could have adopted a victim mentality and coasted as much as he could—only doing enough to get by. Instead, he dedicated himself to excelling in whatever position he was given. The result? "Daniel so distinguished himself among the administrators and the satraps by his exceptional qualities that the king planned to set him over the whole kingdom" (Daniel 6:3).

Daniel's greatness was never about his own advancement in the Babylonian government and society—it was all about representing God well in a foreign country. His deep and abiding work ethic, his sincere integrity, and his wisdom become a testimony to the God that He served.

Walt Disney knew that his name had grown to mean something. It meant family entertainment that was wholesome and engaging for all ages. His name represented the excellent work that he had produced. And when the audience saw his name on a film or a short—they knew they could expect excellence. Walt took this responsibility seriously, as he knew that his work would influence how people from all around the world would perceive his industry.

The Compound Effect of Quality

There's a special thing about excellence: (like faith) it compounds over time. Every act of excellence adds credibility to the next opportunity. Every commitment to quality builds trust that offers more opportunities.

Walt Disney understood and experienced this compounding effect all of his life. Because of the excellence of his earliest Mickey Mouse cartoons, he was able to gamble on Snow White. The popularity of Snow White allowed him to try his hand at Pinocchio, Fantasia, etc. The creativity in his animated films impressed potential investors for Disneyland and even allowed him to expand into live-action films.

But here's the catch: Each project wasn't simply building on the achievement of what came before it—it was raising the bar for what Disney entertainment could be. Walt never believed in resting on one's laurels. He did not rest, but rather he leveraged each victory as a springboard to higher levels of achievement.

As leaders today, we are called to give our best. That means we take all that God has given us—talents, abilities, resources, etc.—and we use them to their fullest. We do the most with what we've got. And we do not do it because we want the praise, we want the cushy reward, or for the thought that "once we get this behind us it will all be easier." When we do our best for God, to achieve the vision that God has given us, then we will have the opportunity to give our best again and again and again. We get the privilege of showing the world what it looks like to be excellent stewards of God's many gifts.

The Innovation Imperative

Walt Disney's dedication to quality did not mean he would do what other people did and strive to match their level of achievement. For Walt doing his best meant attempting to do things that no one else had done before. Walt believed that the route to excellence was paved with creativity and unending innovation.

When Technicolor was available, Walt didn't simply attempt to color in his previous black-and-white animation formula. He reimagined the way one could tell a story with color in "Flowers and Trees," which received the first Academy Award for Best Animated Short Film.

When sound technology came around, Walt didn't just slap dialogue in his cartoons. He revolutionized cinema with Steamboat Willie, inventing the synchronized soundtrack—something approaching a whole new kind of entertainment.

When TV came on the scene, and the other studios feared that it would be the death of movies, Walt embraced the medium. He created the television version of the Mickey Mouse Club (The first Mickey Mouse Club began on June 29, 1929, at the Fox Dome Theatre in Venice, California, and quickly spread across the country and around the world. Kids would gather to watch the Mickey Mouse cartoons on Saturdays before the feature film.), then The Wonderful World of Disney. And Walt didn't just produce The Wonderful World, he was its host, and he would use each show to tell stories in ways that would have been impossible on film.

The dedication to innovation reflected Walt's understanding that the quest for excellence is never over. And today, we live in a fast-paced and ever-changing world—if we are going to pursue excellence then it requires that we be more like Walt, and be nimble and adaptable—always ready to innovate, try, fail, innovate, and try again.

We can find a similar message in the Bible. Jesus, in His Sermon on the Mount, said to His disciples, "Be perfect, therefore, as your Father in Heaven is perfect" (Matt. 5:48). This is not a call for sinless perfection—it is an appeal for progressive sanctification. Just as God's work never ceases as He is always creating and always making things new, we must open ourselves up to the fact that we should always be changing and growing in how we faithfully serve Him and serve each other. In our lives, we must be ready and willing to innovate, change, and grow—if we settle for personal stagnation, how can we lead anyone or anything forward?

The Cost of Excellence

Let me level with you: to be excellent is expensive. It costs more money, more time, more energy, and more emotional effort to be great rather than to settle for whatever you can get as "good enough." Walt Disney learned this lesson the hard way again and again.

Snow White's $1.5 million dollar cost was actually three times its original budget. That's a lot of money!

Fantasia didn't make money at first because audiences weren't prepared for something so artistic in an entertainment medium. Building Disneyland forced Walt to mortgage everything he had. At times, his obsession with excellence nearly drove the company into bankruptcy.

But Walt knew something that most leaders either fail to understand or refuse to believe: the price of excellence is always less than the cost of mediocrity. It might feel like taking shortcuts for temporary cost-savings is a good idea, but it never, ever is because that kind of poor performance destroys your reputation and credibility and poisons future opportunities.

It's the same way with leadership. The additional investment of money and energy to have done it right the first time is always less than what comes from accepting a shoddy job.

This same truth is taught in the Bible but in different words. Let me remind you of what Jesus said about the action taken before construction begins: "Suppose one of you wants to build a tower. Won't you first sit down and estimate the cost to see if you have enough money to complete it? For if you lay the foundation and are not able to finish it, everyone who sees it will ridicule you" (Luke 14:28-29).

Excellence requires an investment at the start, but it also pays dividends for years and is completely worth it. Mediocre may be cheaper in the short run, but it is far more expensive in the long run—missed opportunities, damaged reputations, and work that has to be done over because it was not done right the first time. How many times have we given in to the loud voice saying that there is a faster, cheaper, or easier way. Then, when the results disappoint us and others, we have to spend even more time and resources to do it again and do it right. While we can probably easily calculate the expense of money and time to do a "re-do." What we can't calculate is the disappointment we cause people to feel and the damage to our reputation in their eyes.

Excellence As Service

When Walt Disney "pursued perfection," it wasn't just for his own glory or benefit—it was about how he might serve others. He truly felt that families deserved the best kind of entertainment he could offer. This attitude of service made his drive for excellence a privilege and not a burden.

When you begin to understand that your work is in service to others, the pursuit of excellence becomes a moral obligation rather than a professional preference. Your customers are spending their hard-earned cash on you (or your donors are giving their cash to support your stated purpose) and it should be worth every penny. Your team members who are relying on your leadership deserve your most thoughtful decisions.

This attitude of service reappears throughout Scripture. When Jesus washed the feet of His disciples, it wasn't just a demonstration of humility. He was teaching us how to serve each other.

The Apostle Paul wrote, "Whatever you do, work at it with all your heart, as working for the Lord, not for human masters" (Colossians 3:23). Paul knew that we are to serve the Lord by excelling in our work—even if your supervisor isn't showing the way, or your direct reports aren't stepping up, or your peers don't feel they should bother.

When we are working for God's glory and the sake of others, excellence becomes an act of worship. Everything we do right, every time we solve problems, every time someone benefits from something that we do, it's not JUST about us or the job, it is an act of worship—an offering to the one who blessed us with our gifts, abilities, and resources.

This is something Walt Disney understood (though he never articulated it in spiritual terms). His genius was never a product of an inflated ego, nor did it come from the drive to win; rather, he worked and served with deep gratitude for his gifts, and he felt a responsibility to use them well. He often said he felt privileged to be in the entertainment industry and he wanted his work to reflect that privilege by virtue of its quality.

The Legacy of Excellence

Here's the interesting thing about excellence: It lasts longer than the people who make it. Walt Disney himself passed away in 1966, yet the idea and values upon which he founded his studio continue to guide The Walt Disney Company today. Beyond that, his pursuit of excellence helped to raise the bar for an entire entertainment industry.

As the Disney movies raised the level of animation quality, other studios had to step up or get out. By showing that theme parks could be clean, safe, and family-friendly, Disneyland changed expectations not just for its own operations but also for the broader amusement park industry. When Disney proved that children's programming could be both entertaining and educational, it set the tone for all such programming throughout the industry.

There's no doubt that excellence really does build its own legacy far greater than the moment. When we commit to doing our best work, at any time and in any place, it isn't just about serving the people or community members who are there in front of us—rather, it's about creating expectations for others and setting them up for success beyond that which we had.

The Bible tells us that there is enduring influence, or a lasting legacy, for faithful people who are striving toward excellence in their service to God. Psalm 112:6 says, "For the righteous will never be moved; he will be remembered forever." This isn't about being famous or recognized in worldly ways—it's talking about having an effect down through the centuries through a life lived with excellence and integrity.

Yes, the temple of Solomon was eventually destroyed, but the standard that he set became the basis for Jewish worship for centuries to come. Daniel was in Babylon until the empire fell, but his model of excellence in service has inspired generations of believers to do the same when they are in (or feel like they are in) a foreign land. The end of Paul's missionary journeys culminated with his own death by being beheaded in Rome, but the harvest of seeds he planted as he formed churches across Asia Minor, and the effects of the letters he wrote that are contained in the New Testament all continue to influence the work of ministry in our world even now.

Christian leaders today have an equal opportunity to leave legacies like those too. When we bring our best to work in the roles in which we currently serve, we set the bar high for the others with whom we work or serve. When we serve with excellence people may not recognize it immediately or admit it now willingly, but time will tell and truth will win out—the legacy you leave behind you will be worthy of remembering.

Faith in Action: Personal Application

So how do we establish the commitment to push ourselves and strive for excellence in our leadership journey? And how would we shift from embracing "good enough" to aiming for "greatness?"

First, **connect your work to your worship**. Walt Disney's excellence was driven by his deep belief that entertainment made a difference in the lives of ordinary people. Your choice of excellence should be inspired by the understanding that your work is for God and others.

1. Pray and ask Jesus to help you see your work through His eyes.
2. How do you see your current role serving His kingdom?

3. How does performing your duties with excellence bring honor to Him and benefit others?

When serving God and others through your work is the primary filter you use to view what you do, excellence quickly becomes a byproduct of your faith.

Second, **figure out which standards really count the most**. You don't have to be perfect at everything, but you should strive for excellence in the things that matter—the things that align with your values and move you toward fulfilling your vision.

Walt Disney was a perfectionist about storytelling, animation quality, and guest experience. Those were the areas most reflected in his vision of providing outstanding family entertainment. You'll also want to identify the two to three places in which excellence would help drive your effectiveness and impact over time.

Third, **invest in lifelong learning and development**. Excellence is not a level you reach, it's an adventure in which you live. Walt Disney never stopped learning how to do big new things, develop new techniques, and go ever further with what was possible.

You should commit to continual learning and working to grow in your area of service or responsibility. Read books. Attend conferences. Find mentors. Seek out feedback from people whose opinion you respect. See everything you do as an opportunity to learn more. Each failure can give you feedback, and every success is a building block for something better.

Fourth, **create systems that enable excellence**. You need processes, tools, and habits that make great work an easy regular routine. Develop checklists so you never forget a process, establish quality control systems for your work, employ regular reviews, and then renew your plan for improvement. Create accountability relationships that push you to continue reaching higher standards, doing high-quality work, and striving for excellence (even when you're tired or short of time).

Faith in Action: Leadership Application

Now, let's take a look at what you can do to help foster a culture of excellence within your own team/organization.

Raise the bar and keep it up. There is never a season or even a day to take a vacation from excellence. There is no time when "settling" is acceptable. Walt Disney was notorious for his willingness to throw away work that didn't reach his standards. He wasn't swayed because of how much time or effort had been invested in something that he knew had to go.

Identify what excellence looks like in each of your organization's core parts. If you aren't clear about what excellence in your particular world looks like, you'll never get there. Create examples, rubrics, and other tools that will help people understand what you expect. Include these expectations in your hiring and training processes, as well as in your regular performance reviews.

Reward excellence, not just results. If you want people to actually pursue excellence then make it obvious whenever you notice it—celebrate it and even show your excitement when someone gets close to what you expect. Tell stories about times when someone acted on their belief in excellence and good things happened. Explain to your employees that you appreciate how work gets done, not just what is produced.

Invest in people's ability to truly do excellent work. You can't have excellence without competence and competence requires training, equipment, and support. One of the reasons that Walt Disney founded Disney University was to create a reservoir of potential employees who would understand the company's values and commitment to excellence. Provide training that allows your staff to become better at what they do. Invest in tools, technology, and resources that can make excellent work possible. Establish mentorship programs that pair successful senior performers with those who are developing their abilities.

Show your team how you value excellence in yourself. Your team is waiting to see if you are going to hold yourself accountable to what you expect of them. Demonstrate to your team that quality matters. Share your own dedication to practice and your commitment to growth. Admit when your own work doesn't meet your standards and show that you don't settle for less than the best. Show your team that excellence is the thing you are all journeying toward, not a place at which you or anyone has already arrived.

Create systems which make it easier to excel. You can change your world by developing structures and routines that support and encourage quality. Add design flows with intermittent quality checks. Institute decision making processes that consider long-term effects instead of focusing only on immediate results. Invent new budgeting and scheduling techniques to accommodate and empower excellent work, not just completed work.

The Excellence Mandate

Walt Disney's life story demonstrates in a memorable way that excellence is not just about better products/services, but it's about becoming a better person and helping others become better people. Your willingness to do whatever it takes to be excellent is going to develop you into a stronger person, it will help increase your skills, and it will lay the foundation for future influence and impact.

This is something we should all embrace as believers. After all, Scripture says, whatever you do, "Whether in word or deed, do it all in the name of the Lord Jesus, giving thanks to God the Father through him" (Colossians 3:17). Mediocrity is not acceptable when we do whatever it is we do in Jesus' name. And here is a fact we all have to accept, in all that we do, we carry His name.

The good news is that God is with us. He comes alongside us through the power of the Holy Spirit with wisdom, resources, and connections. He partners with us to help us grow to be our best selves. Our job, in the meantime, is to be a good steward over the gifts that He has given us, so that we can grow in our ability to serve Him and others.

Walt Disney was a man whose dedication to excellence and making the world a better place has resulted in more than could have been imagined. As Christian leaders, we have the opportunity to build something even greater. Our work can mirror God's own character and all that we do can serve His Kingdom purposes.

The question is not whether you should (can) be excellent—God has put such gifts and opportunities in you. The question is whether you will pay the price for excellence. Will you give your all to the hard work necessary for you to be as good as you possibly could be?

Here's some homework before you move on to the next chapter. Answer these questions: What would your leadership look like if you approached everything you did as an opportunity to give glory to God by doing a great job? Where are you settling for "good enough" at work, at home, in relationships, in you? What would it look like to strive for excellence in those places?

Remember, excellence isn't about being perfect; it's about being intentional in giving your all. It is about caring enough to do your best work, continuing to learn, and keeping your sights set on the long view rather than the right now.

CHAPTER SIX

The Magic Happens When We Serve

Servant Leadership and Humility

What do you think Walt Disney was doing early on the morning of July 17, 1955—the day Disneyland first opened? In an executive suite wining and dining dignitaries? Schmoozing with celebrities? No, nothing like that. Walt was walking through the park in his work clothes picking up the trash.

The man who'd just built the most advanced theme park in history, the dreamer who'd reinvented family-friendly entertainment, the boss whose name was on the front gate—he spent the morning of opening day performing what a lot of people would think of as beneath him. And this wasn't a one-time occurrence. Once the park opened, Walt often began his day in the same way.

Later, when a reporter asked Walt about this, he said he got involved in the park because it belonged to the families who went there. He thought that an exceptional guest experience hinged on the details, whether that was him picking up litter, speaking to children in the park, or his addressing problems head on instead of delegating them to someone else.

Now, some of you might say, "Well, that's a nice story, but didn't Walt Disney expect a lot out of his employees because he was a perfectionist?" And you'd be correct—Walt was a hard-driving perfectionist in his pursuit of quality. But here's the amazing thing: his expectations for others were never as high as those he had set for himself. Those who worked with him often said that his leadership style was not, "Do as I say," but rather, "Follow me."

That "follow me" approach is what true servant leadership looks like. It's not a question of being soft or caving or failing to make tough choices. It's about understanding that real leadership isn't about raising yourself up to receive praise and adoration—it is about lifting others up and doing whatever is necessary to be a blessing to them.

The best leaders really are those who use power to empower others to do great things.

The Upside-Down Kingdom

Leadership as Walt Disney knew it, was built on a principle Jesus shared in the first century: "Whoever wants to become great among you must be your servant, and whoever wants to be first must be slave of all" (Mark 10:43-44). And this wasn't simply a well-meaning nugget of advice for kids in Sunday school, it was a radical new idea about authority, one that would completely contradict the way humanity had thought of leadership up to that point!

In Jesus' era, to be a leader was to rule over people from a position of authority, gathering wealth and status for oneself at the expense of the other people. Leaders in Rome led with fear and physical intimidation. Priests imposed their control through complex regulations. Political leaders purchased loyalty through patronage and terror.

Then Jesus came along and did something radical. He washed His disciples' feet. Think about that night in the Upper Room—the night before Jesus was to be crucified. The disciples, who had watched Jesus calm the wind and waves, now watched Him humbling Himself before them to do what only one who is recognized as the lowest servant in a home would be expected to do. Startled, Peter asked, "Lord, are you going to wash my feet?" He was probably just putting into words what everyone else in the room was thinking.

Jesus wasn't simply providing an example of humility as a nice character trait. He was redefining leadership itself. "I have set you an example that you should do as I have done for you," He told them. "Very truly I tell you, no servant is greater than his master, nor is a messenger greater than the one who sent him" (John 13:15-16).

Walt Disney seemed to understand this concept. He had power not because he was the company's founder or because of how much of his personal money he poured into projects. He had power and he had influence because he was willing to work harder than anyone else, care more than anyone else, and even take blame for any problems others had caused.

The Power of Personal Investment

One other thing I've noticed about Walt Disney and his method of leadership is that he never asked someone to do something that he wasn't willing to do himself. If the artists were burning the midnight oil to deliver on a deadline, Walt had his sleeves rolled up joining in sharing ideas, offering suggestions, and working on storyboards— and he'd probably be there later than any of them. And when the crews building Disneyland ran into what seemed like insurmountable problems, Walt would always be there to brainstorm solutions with them.

That was not micromanagement, it was leadership by serving. Walt knew that people would follow someone who made a personal investment in doing things right, not merely barking orders from a safe distance. This reminds me of Nehemiah rebuilding the wall of Jerusalem. When Nehemiah reached Jerusalem and actually saw the damage, he could have set up an office, spread out plans for different contractors, and overseen construction from a safe distance. But instead, he inspected the walls himself, collaborated with the people, shared in the work, and made sure that he shared the vision often.

Nehemiah said to the people, "Come, let us rebuild the wall of Jerusalem, and we will no longer be in disgrace." Notice that he said "us" and "we," not "you." He would participate in the work, not just operate as an overseer. When he received word that the enemies would stop at nothing to strike terror in the workers, he didn't hire bodyguards just to protect himself—he armed his workers and stationed guards to protect them all.

The result? "The people worked with all their heart" (Nehemiah 4:6). Why? Because their leader had shown he was willing to work with all his heart right there beside them.

Walt Disney created that same dynamic at his studio and theme park. Sketch artists pushed because they saw Walt pushing. Construction workers on-site worked with impossible deadlines, because they saw Walt sharing the pressure and the risk. Disneyland employees maintained very high standards of excellence because they watched Walt holding himself to that high level as well.

The Multiplication Effect

Like so many other things we've looked at, the amazing power of servant leadership is that it compounds. When people see and feel real service-based leadership, they start to lead the same way. Servant leadership can spread from the leader throughout the organization.

Walt Disney discovered this during his career. Artists who were schooled in servant leadership and excellence under Walt had the same expectations with their own projects and teams. When Disney Cast Members left to work at other companies or to start their own companies, they couldn't help but take the lessons they learned from Walt with them. Because of this, Walt's philosophy of servant leadership and customer service had a lasting ripple effect not only in the Disney companies, but in the business culture of other organizations as well.

The same multiplication principle is evident in Jesus and His disciples. He didn't merely "teach" them about servant leadership; He lived it out for three years while they watched. The result? After He died on the cross, rose again from the dead, and ascended into heaven, those very same disciples were the ones that literally turned the world upside down as they followed their Master's radical example of servant leadership while spreading the Gospel and planting churches throughout the world.

Peter, who resisted when Jesus stooped to wash his feet, later wrote, "Be shepherds of God's flock that is under your care, watching over them—not because you must, but because you are willing, as God wants you to be; not pursuing dishonest gain, but eager to serve; not lording it over those entrusted to you, but being examples to the flock" (1 Peter 5:2-3). Peter had learned that authentic leadership is about serving others, helping them to succeed and achieve rather than acting solely in the interest of one's own advancement.

The Paradox of Authority

The leadership of Walt Disney illustrates one of the great paradoxes of servant leaders—the more you empower others, the more power you have. The more you invest in the success of others, the more your own successes grow. The more you lead by serving, the more people will follow you. It's counterintuitive in a world that encourages us to hold onto our power, defend our territory, and make sure we get the credit. But that's not the way servant leadership functions, it operates in a different economy, an economy that says, when we put our time and attention into investing in others, we will reap the greatest returns.

Think about how Walt responded to the success he found in Snow White. He could have made it all about himself, leveraged the movie's success, and rebranded himself as the animation king. That wasn't his goal. He even used the profits from the movie to reinvest in his whole team. He used the proceeds to buy better equipment, expand the studio so he could hire more animators, and take on bigger and bigger projects that would provide opportunities for everybody involved.

When Snow White was honored with a special Academy Award, Walt ensured that everyone on staff received recognition. By spreading credit all around, he did exactly the opposite of what many onlookers were expecting—in that moment, he elevated his own reputation and power as a leader.

This principle appears throughout Scripture. It would have been justified for Joseph in the Old Testament to hold a grudge and to plot his revenge against his brothers who had betrayed him (by selling him into slavery) when he was Egypt's second-in-command. Instead, he used his power to spare their lives and the lives of the members of their families. "You intended to harm me," he told them, "But God intended it for good to accomplish what is now being done, the saving of many lives" (Genesis 50:20).

Joseph could have used his power just to achieve his own goals, but that is not what power is about.

Joseph's servant leadership approach didn't diminish his power, it multiplied it. His brothers and their children were to be blessed solely because of the mercy and generosity shown them. Joseph's power was not for him; he used it to bless others.

The Discipline of Development

One of the greatest aspects of Walt Disney's dedication to servant leadership was his passion to help bring out the full potential in other people. He didn't just hire talented people, he invested in increasing their talent, skills, and abilities. He didn't just delegate tasks, he assigned tasks to help people stretch and grow.

Walt's emphasis on continuing education and personal development was something he took so seriously that he was willing to make it a priority. Walt spent countless hours reviewing people's work, giving them very specific feedback, and providing ways for them to learn even more with Disney University and other channels for development.

I know that you may be thinking that this was a self-serving action on Walt's part. After all, when his staff developed, they would then be able to help him accomplish his vision. While that is true, that wasn't the driving force. Walt sincerely wanted to help people grow. He had a deep desire to see people do well. Walt felt that the most fundamental duty of leadership was to help others achieve their highest potential.

This really is the same model for growth that Jesus Himself had with His disciples. He didn't select unusually talented people. He selected individuals with a sprig of talent and then spent three years ensuring that their small gift blossomed. He gave them hands-on learning, provided feedback, and helped them navigate through mistakes and successes.

When Jesus was about to ascend into heaven, there was no comprehensive manual left behind, and no intricate org chart. He ultimately left twelve men (okay, eleven after Judas, but then they added Matthias and later Paul joined the group—so, I guess that's thirteen) that He had influenced—people who had experienced His servant leadership—these were the people who would follow His example and would multiply His impact in the world.

Paul continued this developmental tradition in his ministry. He wasn't just planting churches—he was raising up leaders who could plant other churches. Not only did he write letters, but he also trained Timothy, Titus, and others in how to build and lead healthy Christian communities.

Paul's model for developing leaders is summarized in his guidance to Timothy, "The things you have heard me say in the presence of many witnesses entrust to reliable people who will also be qualified to teach others" (2 Timothy 2:2). This is multiplication leadership—inspiring believers and empowering leaders who go out and inspire other believers and empowers other leaders.

The Vulnerability of Service

I will be honest with you, being a servant leader is vulnerable work. Disappointment and heartbreak can happen when you love deeply enough to personally invest in someone else's growth. You become connected to their successes as well as their failures. So, that does expose you somewhat, and you must be ready for that.

Walt Disney faced it at every turn during his career life. He cared so deeply about his team that it left him vulnerable for the times when they let him down. He found the 1941 animators' strike particularly difficult, because he felt personally betrayed by many of the people whose careers he'd helped launch and develop. While he always wanted his team to grow and succeed, it was hard when some of his protégés created rival studios. It was also difficult when people would use the skills they learned at Disney to find opportunities that would serve them, not a higher mission.

You might think that it would be natural (and maybe even expected) that someone like Walt, who invested so much into others, to become guarded or watchful in order to protect himself. However, ultimately, he never did. The only change that came was he became more selective about who he went all in on. But he never stopped believing in people or caring about their development.

I'm going to be honest with you—I find this hard to do. When I was younger, I remember hearing someone say, "Fool me once, shame on you. Fool me twice, shame on me." While I truly want to invest in others and help them grow and develop—I have had moments when people I poured into for years turned their backs on me to advance their own agendas. So, this is now a growth area for me. To remember that investing myself to help someone reach the potential that God has placed in them is more important than me or my feelings.

Also, I know that what I have experienced is nothing compared to Jesus. After three years of calling and personal investment, Judas betrayed Him. They had walked together, eaten and camped together—Judas had witnessed more miracles and heard more teachings than are even recorded in the Bible, and yet he turned on Jesus for thirty pieces of silver.

Then there are the joyful throngs that shouted out His praises when He entered Jerusalem on a donkey's colt but turned into the angry mob that shouted for His crucifixion a few days later.

And what about His disciples, His friends and companions who turned away, didn't show up, or were more concerned about their own safety—when He needed them most.

But Jesus didn't react to betrayal and abandonment with cynicism or self-protection. He even prayed from the cross, "Father, forgive them; for they do not know what they are doing" (Luke 23:34). And, while you may read that as His prayer for the Romans or the Jewish religious establishment, I think that prayer covers us all.

Jesus was the leader who washed His disciples' feet— His commitment to servant leadership was stronger than the hurts He faced.

This vulnerability is one of the things that makes being a servant so powerful. When you allow people to know that you truly care about them, that you are willing to invest in their success, and that you lead from a place of service, you have the chance to make an impact in their lives that will change their world and could change the world.

The Long-Term Perspective

Walt Disney led people with servant leadership but did so always with an eye to the long-term. He had to look past the short-term gains or self-recognition in order to put in the time and energy to help someone else develop. He knew that building people doesn't happen overnight, that greatness takes time and patience, and that to make an impact you have to focus on what will matter years or decades in the future.

It was that long view that allowed Walt to invest in projects and people who wouldn't pay off immediately. Disney University was a costly endeavor to create; it didn't make money it just cost money. When Walt was spending time investing in the nurturing of young animators, he was willing to put off some of his own creative work. Also, when he decided to reinvest his profit into better machinery, facilities, and technology so that the younger animators could grow in their skills and abilities, he was willing to spend the money even when it diminished his personal gain.

Walt fully understood that servant leadership is about making an investment that would last long after the time of your leadership. Walt was building a culture, assembling a team, and establishing standards that were to be kept long after he was gone.

The Bible repeatedly calls on leaders to have that long-term view as well. Moses spent forty years helping the Israelites become a nation and prepare to move into the Promised Land. He knew that he would not be the one who would lead them across the Jordan, but he still gave his all. Joshua also invested in the next generation, helping them get ready for what lay ahead. He knew that the full conquest of Canaan would be drawn out, and he knew that it would take longer than his limited time. When you want the vision to continue—the goal to be achieved— you must invest in others who will take up the ball and keep running to the end zone.

The Apostle Paul had a goal to create self-sustaining bodies of believers. He said to the Thessalonians, "You know how we lived among you for your sake. You became imitators of us and of the Lord" (1 Thessalonians 1:5-6). Paul was never trying to micro-manage the congregations he launched—he truly wanted them to reach the point where they could flourish on their own.

What we need today from Christian leaders is that same long-term perspective. It's not just about what results we achieve today or this quarter, or personal success. We have to think about what can be accomplished when we lift people up, build cultures, and create patterns that will eventually bear fruit for generations.

The Ecosystem of Excellence

Walt Disney's servant leadership, one might say, built an ecosystem of excellence—a work environment in which everyone was expected to bring their A game. The work world he created nurtured people, nurtured learning, and was truly a nurturing environment.

This ecosystem didn't happen accidentally. Walt deliberately fostered systems, processes, and relationships to underpin servant leadership throughout the organization. He established mentorship programs, opened siloed doors between departments, and installed feedback loops that allowed people to learn and grow.

More importantly, however, Walt showed everyone how he wanted every member of the team to behave. He modeled that authority exists for serving, excellence is to be used for the benefit of others, and success is to be measured by what is accomplished by the team, not individuals.

A similar environment was created by Jesus with His disciples. He let them develop as He taught them through parables and conversations. He sent them out to serve in His name and prepared them for the day when He would no longer be with them.

When Jesus directed the seventy-two disciples to enter villages and serve, He wasn't just giving them work, He was creating a context for servant leadership to be modeled, practiced, and reproduced. Jesus used their experiences to teach the entire group lessons when they returned to describe what took place.

This ecosystem mentality was also preserved in the early church. Acts 2:42-47 describes a community "devoted to the apostles' teaching and to fellowship, to the breaking of bread and to prayer." This was not merely a description of worship practices, but it was also a picture of an ecology in which servant leadership could be nurtured and sustained.

The Paradox of Influence

Which brings us to one of the Walt Disney paradoxes, and this is truly unique. Quite often Walt exercised his maximum influence with his team when he worked very hard to stay out of the spotlight. I know that we watch the Wonderful World of Disney and see his pictures all over the place, we think that it was "All Walt—All the Time." But it wasn't that way on a day-to-day basis. While so many other entertainment executives worked hard to get attention, fame, and awards, Walt deeply cared about the quality of what he was producing, and he wanted to build others up and let them take the credit.

The result? The influence of Walt extended beyond his company, and even the industry. Disney movies molded global culture, setting a standard for what family fare should look like, and the power of those images lingers. Disneyland, Disney parks, Disney resorts, Disney cruise ships, etc. have transformed the concept of service in the hospitality industry. The Disney method of developing employees caught on across a variety of industries and is the basis for the Disney Institute today.

As a leader, when your goal is to be of service to your team and to others, and not just to get ahead, you're typically more effective than leaders whose main focus is on their own kudos and promotion. Leaders who are focused on themselves will find it very difficult to serve others as you climb over them on the ladder of success.

Jesus demonstrated this principle throughout His ministry. He would frequently ask those whom He healed not to make known what He had done for them. He retreated from the masses who sought to crown Him king. He was always deflecting attention from Himself to His Father, and the needs of the individuals to whom He ministered.

On the whole, Jesus was and is more influential than any human leader. For two millennia, His teaching of servant leadership has inspired billions to bear these same things in their friendships and duties. Paul exhibited the goal of all Christians when he identified himself in Romans 1:1 as "a servant of Christ Jesus," and nothing more.

What made Jesus and Paul influential was not a lust for validation. It was their sense of devotion to the needs of people—and the need to help bring out the potential in other people. Their legacy was to be the reproduction of their servant leader values in the lives of those in whom they had invested.

The Integration of Character and Competence

Perhaps the single most remarkable trait of Walt Disney as a servant leader was his ability to merge high-performance expectations with caring deeply for people. He was one of the hardest bosses in Hollywood and one of the most loyal. He demanded the best of his team—and he invested in their ability to deliver.

It is here that the balance of character and competence becomes all-important in effective servant leadership. It's not enough merely to be nice to people, if you're not helping push them forward so they can get meaningful results. It doesn't work to demand a high performance if you aren't offering the support and encouragement that people need to step up and achieve.

Walt struck this balance by setting clear expectations, investing in people, and helping the team to see his personal pursuit of excellence. People understood what he wanted, why it mattered, and saw how hard he was willing to work to get where we were all hoping to go.

This blend of prayer and leadership was the trademark of King David's rule. He was a mighty warrior, who showed no mercy to Israel's enemies, and yet he was also called "a man after God's own heart" and loved his followers greatly.

David's men got thirsty once in battle and almost got themselves killed getting David some water from a well in enemy territory. David's response epitomizes the heart of servant leadership: He refused to drink it; he poured it out as an offering to God. He didn't feel worthy to drink something that his men had paid a high price to obtain. David's action shows us that servant leadership takes into consideration the sacrifices of other people.

The Courage of Confrontation

One thing that we need to keep in mind about servant leadership is it is not about avoiding the tough conversations and necessary confrontations. Walt Disney was known for his blunt criticism of work, his readiness to throw out work that didn't measure up, and pressure in pursuit of excellence even when it caused tension.

But Walt did not confront people in the usual authoritarian sense. He criticized the work, not the person. The corrections came with coaching and development. His high expectations were paired with high support and personal investment in people's success.

This is a perfectly biblical view of confrontation. Jesus was direct about how you could or should grow, but it was rooted in love. And the purpose of the criticism was restoration, not punishment.

Jesus did not humiliate, embarrass, and belittle Peter when He confronted him about denying Him. He asked him three times whether he loved Him and was devoted to Him and then said, "Feed my sheep" (John 21:15-17). In other words, instead of destroying their relationship, the challenge became a stage upon which Peter could be restored, trained, and developed for service.

Paul also went on to rebuke problems in churches that were formed by him. What He writes to the Corinthians, he reveals divisions, immorality, and theological confusion. Yet Paul's reprimand is spoken out of love and with the well-being and growth of the church in mind.

"I am writing this not to shame you but to warn you as my dear children," Paul wrote to the Corinthians. "Even if you had ten thousand guardians in Christ, you do not have many fathers, for in Christ Jesus I became your father through the gospel" (1 Corinthians 4:14-15).

Servant leadership is having the courage to be honest and direct. But to do so in a way that focuses on the results, not the person.

Faith in Action: Personal Application

So how do we "scale" this form of servant leadership as we evolve on our own journey to being more effective leaders? What would it be like to move from selfish leadership to selfless leadership?

First, **clarify your motivation for leading**. Walt Disney's servant leadership was effective because he truly enjoyed bringing joy and magic to families, which translated into developing excellence in his team. Your servant leadership should be rooted in your vision and fueled by your genuine concern for those you are called to lead.

Honestly ask yourself why you want to lead or be in a leadership position. What is driving you? Do you want to get ahead, be recognized for what you have achieved? Or do you get out of bed every morning because it provides an opportunity to make someone's life a little bit better than it is without you, and you can help them accomplish things with even greater purpose?

Ask God to give you a heart for the people in your workplace. Pray by name and by role for each of your staff, asking God to show you how you can assist them in becoming ever more productive, and how you can help them grow to reach their potential.

When you stop asking questions like, "How can my position help me?" and you begin asking, "What can I do to add value to other people through this position?" That is when you know you are well on the road to servant leadership.

Second, **cultivate the habit of being personally invested in the lives of others**. Servant leadership must allow time and energy to grow the potential in others.

Just pick two to three people you already have in your orbit who are ripe to grow. Commit yourself to investing in their growth by regular mentorship discussions, challenging and stretching assignments, thoughtful feedback, and continuous learning.

This investment will take time away from your own actions and energy which could be applied toward achieving your own dreams and accomplishing your own agenda. But, as Walt Disney learned, the reward of building others over time is far greater than the investment we must make in our own development.

Third, **practice the art of empowerment**, rather than control. Servant leaders invest in building the capacity of other people to thrive and they do not demand absolute control over every decision and outcome.

Look for ways to delegate meaningful work to people you are developing. Provide them every form of assistance and resources they need to succeed, but, again, do not fall into the trap of micromanaging. If they fail, consider that part of the learning process rather than simply taking back control.

Remind yourself, empowerment is a journey, not an event. Start slowly with fewer responsibilities and delegate more as people demonstrate they are capable of doing the job and also have a strong character. The goal is to create people who can eventually operate without you, perhaps even better than you do.

Fourth, **bring vulnerability and authenticity to your relationships**. For servant leadership, you must have the courage to be real about your experiences, struggles, and learning processes.

Share with the team similar struggles in your current work or ministry, so they see leadership is a journey and not a destination. Acknowledge when you are wrong and demonstrate your ability to correct your course. Seek feedback from where you lead and take what they say seriously.

This kind of vulnerability doesn't make you weaker—it makes you stronger, because people believe that you are committed to the same ethos of openness and growth that they want to align themselves with.

Faith in Action: Leadership Application

Now that you know the advantages, let's see how you can weave servant leadership principles into your company culture.

Create systems that serve people's development rather than just organizational efficiency.

Walt Disney didn't open Disney University because it was the most cost-efficient way to train employees, he did so because it was the most effective way to unlock their potential.

Through the lens of employee development, assess your existing organizational systems. Are your performance review and goal-setting processes rewarding growth or just checking the box? Are your training programs building people's capability or just checking a box on basic job requirements? Do your criteria for promotion value servant leadership characteristics or do they only merely reward personal success?

Reconceive systems that prioritize the growth of the individual, not just organizational results. That may mean investing more time and money in formal training, mentorship programs, or career development paths that value developing others.

Create a culture of leadership as service rather than position of power! This will mean being more intentional in the communication, demonstration, and reinforcement of servant leadership principles.

Make it a point to talk in leadership meetings regularly about decisions and how they will impact the development and success of your team members.

When you are going through the interview process, consider if the candidates are dedicated to developing others on the top of their technical skill set. In reward programs, celebrate leaders who sacrificed for net team triumphs over individual accomplishment.

Emphasize that leaders serve.

Create measurement systems that track how well servant leadership is working. If you want a servant leadership culture, measure and reward servant leadership behaviors.

Integrate 360-degree feedback into leadership evaluation, where team members score how well they think their leader is working to support their development and success. Create metrics to track not only what a leader achieves, but how they achieve it, and how they develop others along the way.

Track signs like employee development, team commitment, and retention of top performers— and how often people from leaders' teams are promoted. These measures will be instrumental in identifying and advancing the people who are genuinely committed to helping others succeed.

Model servant leadership personally while developing other servant leaders around you. The culture of your organization will look like how you lead. Demonstrate servant leadership and seek out other leaders who demonstrate these qualities.

Provide opportunities for emerging servant leaders to apply these principles with proper support and feedback. Establish a system of succession planning focused on both technical competencies and character and the qualities of servant leadership. The goal—and hope—is to create a leadership pipeline populated by people who know that authority exists to serve others, not the other way around.

The Servant Leadership Legacy

The servant leadership of Walt Disney made a staggering impact around the world in more ways than just entertainment. His commitment to families was instrumental in shaping the children-oriented programming that the global culture takes for granted today. His focus on the development of his staff shaped how business was conducted over numerous professions. His passion for excellence in customer service was visionary and raised the bar of the hospitality industry.

But perhaps more than anything, his servant leadership style rubbed off on tens of thousands of those who worked under him then took that ethos to their own organizations and their own communities. The sum of all this: his servant leadership has left a mark on the lives of many who may never watch a Disney film or walk through a Disney park.

It's this kind of multiplication that Scripture promises for servant leaders. "Whoever serves me must follow me; and where I am, my servant also will be. Him will my Father honor" (John 12:26). We get to participate in God's most important work of growing people and expanding His purposes in His Kingdom when we serve others as ourselves.

It's not a matter of whether you will get the chance to practice servant leadership—you will. Every encounter you have with another person is an opportunity to serve someone for their benefit, growth, or happiness. So, the question is—when these moments arise—will you concentrate on yourself and your accolades, or will you focus on serving others?

Walt Disney proved to the world that servant leadership is not just a warm-fuzzy philosophy for Sunday mornings, it's an incredibly practical model that delivers extraordinary results over and over and over again. When we become more intentional about allowing others to be great (as counterintuitive as this may seem), more often than not, we see our influence and impact expand—far beyond what would have been possible had we led solely for self.

And as Christian leaders, we have the ultimate model of servanthood in Jesus Christ. We have the power of the Holy Spirit to give us the strength to love people authentically, to serve sacrificially, and to grow people with the kind of patience and wisdom that far exceeds our natural capacity.

The magic happens—it really does—when we serve. Not because service is some kind of mystical thing in and of itself, but because of the way that God made relationships to work best—both with organizations and human beings—through servant leadership.

So, ponder this: What would change if, instead of everything being about supporting (even hiding behind) your ego, every task was a chance to serve others' success?

And let's remember that the greatest amongst us are those who serve. That's not just wisdom from the Bible, it turns out to be the secret of leadership that really changes the world.

CHAPTER SEVEN

The Magic Kingdom of Leadership

Bringing It All Together

On December 15, 1966, Walt Disney was sixty-five years old and hospitalized at St. Joseph's Hospital in Burbank just across the street from his studio. Just weeks before, he had been excitedly planning his most ambitious project yet, EPCOT (Experimental Prototype Community of Tomorrow), a futuristic city that would showcase how technology and human ingenuity could find better ways to live together. He was also planning what would become Walt Disney World in Orlando, Florida; Mineral King, a resort area in California's Sierra Nevada Mountains; and Riverfront Square, an initiative in Missouri since his happiest days were those he spent in Marceline when he was young.

He was in his last days, but he never stopped inspiring, he didn't stop teaching, he continued to remind those around him about his vision, and he kept focused on the principles that were important to him. When he spoke with people from the studio, with family, and friends, he didn't list regrets or fret over wasting his life as many do in those moments. He simply wanted everyone to continue the work he had begun, to hold to the standards he had set, and to never forget the end goal—that everything he had done and was doing was about serving families and providing them with wholesome, quality entertainment that would bring joy and magic to their lives.

When Roy Disney, his elder brother and business partner, made a final visit to him, Walt was less worried about his own life than he was about the lives of others. Roy would need to recall his vision and the principles he had formulated. He used the ceiling grids as his map to assist Roy in comprehending exactly what he saw as EPCOT. Ultimately, Roy would have to focus his efforts. He was not Walt, he was not the creative genius, so Roy abandoned the plans for Mineral King and Riverfront Square to focus on what he would name Walt Disney World in Orlando. He did this because he knew that Walt was building it to produce the revenue for EPCOT. EPCOT was Walt's next big dream, and Roy wanted to set the stage to accomplish it. So, on October 1, 1971, Roy opened Walt Disney World. Unfortunately, he never saw EPCOT come to fruition as he died on December 20, 1971.

Even as he was faced with death, Walt found his heart drawn to still helping others and seeking to protect everything that had made his accomplishments possible.

The Foundation That Changes Everything

Now, let's go back to where our journey started—that bench in Griffith Park by the carousel, where Walt sat while his daughters rode, laughed, and waved. It was there that Walt first had the vision that would forever change the world of entertainment. But after we have been on Walt's journey of leadership together, I want you to notice something behind that moment.

Walt didn't just dream up a brand-new kind of amusement park. He saw that there was a need, that he had an opportunity to help families, that he could create something great, and that he needed to take a risk for worthwhile goal. That moment on that bench truly contained all of the leadership principles we have been looking at throughout our time together. Vision based upon mission and purpose; faith and trust to believe in the impossible; courage and a willingness to take risks; perseverance and tenacity to go through obstacles not around them in pursuit of excellence; quality in everything; a commitment to serve others well; and the humility to not make it all about himself.

This synthesis of principles was what made Walt Disney a successful leader and why his legacy endures. It wasn't just that he possessed some of the qualities—he somehow made them mesh and rebound off each other in a single integrated whole.

Vision and Purpose were his North Star and song of his life. Just as Abraham set off for a land he did not know when he left Ur, so was Walt ready to fight for a vision and purpose that existed only within him—because they served something bigger than himself.

It was the **Faith and Trust** in which he could not see that gave him power to progress toward what was unfamiliar. Just as David had the audacity to face Goliath armed only with his slingshot and stones, Walt was willing, time and again, to put it all on the line because he had faith that quality would win in the end, and he trusted that it would find its audience.

Courage and Risk-taking helped him have the strength to launch into the unknown—to dare to do the unprecedented. Just as Esther would go to the king to save her people, Walt was willing to risk everything so that he could fulfill what he felt was his purpose.

Perseverance and Resilience gave him the stamina to carry on when the going was tough. Like Job persevering in his faith in God through all of his trials and afflictions, or like Nehemiah who was determined to rebuild the walls in the face of resistance, Walt understood that a breakthrough would never happen, a goal would never be met, a vision would never become a reality, if you threw up your hands and quit.

Excellence and Quality were the norm for him, which put everything he did into a class of its own. Just as Bezalel built the tabernacle and Solomon's builders constructed the temple, Walt understood that if you are making something that impacts people on a great scale then anything less than your best is not just wrong, it is immoral.

Servant Leadership and Humility provided the opportunities that fueled everything else. Similarly to Jesus washing His disciples' feet or Paul identifying himself as a servant of Christ, Walt realized that genuine leadership is about serving other people, and not about them serving you.

The Compound Effect of Integration

What strikes me about Walt Disney as a leader is this: every rule informed the next. His vision was more compelling because it was grounded in service to families and others. His faith became more sustainable because it was directed toward worthy ends, rather than in service of his own needs. His courage was not unregenerate recklessness, it was effective and disciplined excellence. His perseverance was more meaningful because it was about something other than himself—it was about serving others.

This integration is thoroughly biblical. When Jesus called His disciples to follow Him, He didn't give them a leadership development checklist. He called them to live a life in which love, service, courage, faith, and excellence all work together for the advancement of God's Kingdom purposes.

Consider how these worked in concert in the life of the Apostle Paul:

- His vision and purpose were as clear as day: to take the Gospel to the Gentiles and found churches all across the Roman Empire.
- His faith was deep enough that he truly believed that God would bring about the desired end, whatever happened.
- He was fearless. He persisted in preaching despite the imprisonment, the beatings, and the backlash.
- His perseverance was incredible. He kept his eyes on the prize and stayed focused on his ministry even through decades of hardship.
- He was genuinely a servant leader. He constantly looked for ways to help other people rather than himself.

Paul did not develop these virtues in isolation—they built on one another to become a pattern of leadership that transformed the world.

Walt Disney did something similar in his secular world. Every principle that guided him built on another and led to a style of leadership that was extremely effective, and also extremely lasting.

The Legacy Test

Now, as we process all of this, we move to what I'll call "The Legacy Test." It is a test that Walt Disney, among others, passed with flying colors. It's the test that biblical leaders like David, Daniel, and Paul knocked out of the park. And it's the test that every Christian leader faces at some point in his or her journey.

The Legacy Test asks us: **What will survive you when you're done?**

Will the organizations you led still mirror the values that defined you? Will the people you have developed and invested in continue to grow and serve others well? Will the principles that you established still guide others in determining what is right and what is wrong? Will your culture attract and generate more high-performing leaders?

In many ways, Walt Disney aced the Legacy Test. It's been almost sixty years or so since his death and the Disney teams are still working to fulfill his vision (Yes, they wander from it at times, but when they get it right— the joy and the magic are there.). Disney theme parks in America and around the world continue to honor the cleanliness, safety, and service protocols he established. Disney employees are still taught to adhere to the values and principles he found most important. His namesake company continues to attract fresh talent who feel the same way about raising the bar in entertainment.

But Walt's legacy is about so much more than the company he built. His influence in entertainment raised the bar for everyone else. His devotion to customer service rewrote the rules for how many companies operate. His commitment to innovation has been an inspiration for countless entrepreneurs and creators. His servant leadership, the style with which he led and added value to everyone who worked for him, has inspired countless people to take that approach to work into their own careers and communities.

But, most of all, Walt's spirit lives in the millions and millions of families who have enjoyed—and are still enjoying today—Disney entertainment. Children have grown up on Disney movies. Parents share special Disney experiences and magical moments with their kids. Families—now generations of families—have treasured memories at Disney theme parks, cruises, resorts, etc.

That's the kind of legacy that matters. It is impact that reaches beyond your direct involvement, influence that is amplified in the lives of the people you serve, and lasting principles that echo as a blessing long after your time is past.

Your Leadership Legacy

Again, I'll ask you the Legacy Test question: **What will survive you when you're done?**

No, I don't ask the question to be morbid or dramatic, but knowing what legacy you seek to leave either after you die, after you retire, after you move to a new opportunity, after your children grow up and move out, is crucial if you want to lead well now. The decisions you make, the people you develop, the standards you set, and the culture you create all contribute to the legacy (whether positive or not) you are leaving behind whether you realize it or not.

From the outset, Walt Disney was careful about his legacy. He believed entertainment influences culture; great work inspires others to greatness; and servant leadership is a seed that grows in the lives of those who experience it first-hand.

Christians leaders have an opportunity to extend even longer legacies since our work is part of God's eternal Kingdom purposes. As we integrate and apply biblical leadership concepts into our jobs, organizations, families, churches, or communities we are doing more than building/leading a business/organization/ministry/family, we are stewarding opportunities to advance the Kingdom of God and take care of the people whom God loves.

The legacy question is always one of the toughest ones we face. When I started thinking about it, I took a long, critical look at my entire life. Reflecting on my shortcomings as a husband, father, grandfather, pastor, leader, friend, mentor, etc. Then, at the point where I was really ready to apologize to the world for using resources but not producing benefits, I realized that I had been doing it wrong. You can't build legacy that you'll leave tomorrow (or someday) by living in yesterday.

Yes, it's true, we all have a past, and that past is filled with good days and bad, good decisions and bad, times when we were fulfilling our vision and times when we were as blind as bat, moments when we were servant leaders and moments when we were selfish leaders, periods where we excelled and raised the bar, and periods when we were phoning it in at best. We all have a past, but the past good or the bad cannot be our obsession. It can inform us—tell us what we need to do more of—or what we never need to do again, but we can't relive it—we can only learn from it.

Here is a truth you must remember: Your legacy is ahead of you. So, your legacy shaping starts now.

Consider how each of the principles we have discussed will enable you to leave a worthwhile legacy:

Vision and Purpose: When you lead with phenomenal, crystal-clear God-honoring vision it enables others to visualize how their work can contribute to meaningful outcomes. This means the multiplying effect could cause a ripple effect across many institutions and communities.

Faith and Trust: When you demonstrate decision-making based on faith, you're teaching others that God is trustworthy even at times when the outcomes are unknown. This Christian perspective helps others consider issues, react to opportunities, and navigate relationships in their own lives.

Courage and Risk-taking: When you demonstrate thoughtful courage in your pursuit of noble causes, you give permission to attempt big things for God's Kingdom. You inspire others to be courageous when you are courageous. You motivate people to take a risk for a worthwhile cause when they see that lived out in your leadership.

Perseverance and Resilience: When hard things come and you do not compromise on what's important to you, when you don't water down your beliefs, when you don't sidestep your values, you are showing that God's trustworthiness will always outweigh any setback or hardship. Your dedication to what you know is right will inspire others to hang on when things are hard.

Excellence and Quality: When you're working to achieve excellence every single day, then that becomes the new norm that everyone else starts striving toward. Excellent becomes the communal goal and not the exception. Yes, you enjoy the benefit of this influence on your team and environment, but in addition, excellence multiplies as its impact radiates outward through your team.

Servant Leadership and Humility: When you genuinely focus on helping other people to grow, and everyone around you to succeed, the results scale far beyond the sum of your actions. When people are led by true servant leaders, the result often is that they become servant leaders as well.

The Integration Challenge

So, before we close, let me leave you with an actionable challenge that can help transform the effectiveness of your leadership. Choose one area where you'll better implement these six principles in your current role as a leader.

Don't try to change everything at once. If you try to make wide sweeping changes across all areas of personal and professional leadership, you are setting yourself up for frustration and failure. Trying to do it all at once is a sure-fire way to get overwhelmed and do nothing—trust me, I see it happen to many people so many times. I've done it more times than I can count. So, just change one thing at a time.

One situation, one relationship, or one responsibility where you can apply these principles and change for the better.

For Example:

If you face a difficult decision, apply vision (How does this serve our purpose?), trust (How can I trust God for uncertain ends?), courage (Am I brave enough to do what's right rather than what's easy?), perseverance (Will I battle through and stay with it?), excellence (Is this the best we can think and plan?), and servant leadership (How does this benefit others and not just myself?).

If you are developing a team member, apply vision (How does their development serve our mission?), faith (Do I believe in their promise despite slow-er-than-hoped-for progress?), courage (Do I have the courage to have tough conversations and to give honest feedback?), perseverance (Will I per-sist despite the development taking longer than expected?), excellence (Am I helping them get to their very best work as opposed to just okay work?), and servant leadership (Is this about them growing rather than me getting credit for their growth?).

If you are starting something new, use vision (Does this move us closer to fulfilling our God-given purpose?), faith (Do I have confidence in God's provision over and above what I see?), courage (Am I up for going for something big rather than just playing it safe?), perseverance (Am I ready to deal with the inevitable challenges?), excellence (Are we interested in doing this well, or just in getting it done?), and servant leadership (Will this benefit others rather than just elevate me?).

The magic of integrated leadership is that each principle builds upon the others, creating a force and success that no one element can achieve on its own.

The Invitation to Excellence

As we complete this journey together, I'd like to extend to you the same invitation that Walt Disney heard internally as he sat on that bench in Griffith Park—The invitation to strive for excellence, to apply yourself in service to others, to take worthwhile risks, and build something of lasting value that will continue bringing joy and magic to people long after you're gone.

This is not an invitation intended only for media/entertainment moguls or theme park visionaries. It is an invitation offered to every Christian leader who wants to connect biblical lessons to their leadership practices. It is an invitation for all who opt to serve others rather than focus on their personal glory. And it is an invitation for anyone who wants to operate at a level of excellence so that their leadership is truly an act of stewardship and worship.

It doesn't matter if you are leading a Fortune 500 company or a small ministry, running a large department or running a crew of just a few folks, pastoring a mega-church or volunteering your time at the local non-profit, the principles we have explored are applicable to where you are today. The scope may be more limited or broader, but the Kingdom-advancing potential is just as significant wherever you are.

The Invitation Includes:

The opportunity to cast vision that paints a picture that allows people to see how what they do is participating in God's vision for the world. Any task, no matter how unimportant it may seem, can have a purposeful outcome if you see it in the perspective of Kingdom service.

The privilege of displaying faith that tells others that God can be trusted when everything is not yet clear. Such faith-based decision making becomes a testimony that guides others in how they face challenges and opportunities over the course of their lives.

The opportunity to embody courage and to lead others in doing great things for God's Kingdom. It's your willingness to take thoughtful risks that give the people around you the freedom to leave their comfort zones in pursuit of worthy goals.

The chance to demonstrate courage by being patient and enduring challenges. This vividly shows others that you trust in God's steadfast grip on you.

The call to persevere through adversity. Knowing that, when you do, you show that setbacks don't have to equal defeats.

The calling to do excellent work that glorifies God and benefits others. Your pursuit of excellence creates new standards that affect everyone in your circle of influence.

The joy of practicing servant leadership, multiplying your impact through the lives of those whom you grow and empower. What you invest in others is multiplied and goes on long after your direct involvement ends.

The Walt Disney Challenge

The final challenge is what I like to term the Walt Disney Challenge in Christian leadership language:

Take care of people: Who are the people that God has given you—placed in your life—put in your sphere of influence? How can you help them develop, give them tools to succeed, or enhance their wellbeing? How would your leadership change if you saw every meeting and encounter as an opportunity to make God's love visible?

Remember your vision and purpose: What is it that God wants you to accomplish in your current job/role? In what ways does your work contribute to His eternal purposes daily? What shifts in priorities would you need to make to have the greatest Kingdom impact?

Keep the magic alive: How can you keep that sense of wonder and excitement about taking part in God's work? What can you do to help people understand this joy—the satisfaction of using their gifts for significant purposes? What would be different in your leadership energy if you remembered that you're part of the grandest adventure ever to take place in the universe—God's redemption and restoration of His creation?

The Beginning, Not the End

As we reach the end of the book, I'd like to remind you that it is in fact a beginning, not an ending. Walt Disney knew that each finished project was just fertilizer for the next, and every accomplishment was a platform from which to try something even bigger.

This is true for your leadership journey as well. The ideas we've learned aren't just interesting things to think about—they are things that you can use. And the examples aren't simply stories to keep in memory—they are templates to apply to your own situation and battle.

The issue is not whether these principles will work for you—there are, of course, no guarantees—even though they have worked consistently well for those who have honored and applied them in difficult real-world situations. They are based on biblical wisdom and informed by the experience of leaders throughout history who have effectively dealt with bold complex challenges.

The question is whether you will have the faith to implement them, whether you will have the courage to keep doing it when it's hard, whether you will have the perseverance to keep doing it when you don't yet see results, whether you will have the commitment to do your best so that the excellence in your efforts honors God, and if you will serve others, making it about other people's success and not just your own.

The life of Walt Disney teaches that when you take these principles and apply them consistently over a period of time, you can truly accomplish things that seem to be impossible. You can build institutions that serve others with excellence. You can develop people who multiply your influence. You can leave a legacy of service that remains long after you are gone.

But, more than that, Walt reminds us that the journey—that daily choice to serve others, to soar with excellence, to trust faith, to show courage in the face of challenges and uncertainty—is every bit as rewarding as any destination we reach.

Your Magic Kingdom Awaits

Walt Disney constructed magic kingdoms where families could have fun, feel wonder, and be together. As a Christian leader you can potentially create something even greater. A kingdom legacy that emulates God's heart and advances His purposes in the world.

Your "magical kingdom" might be a business that conducts itself with integrity and puts smiles on customers' faces. It may be a ministry that produces leaders, serves the community effectively, and transforms lives. It could be a family that communicates and enacts God's love in their church, community, their work, and around the world.

In the grand scheme of things, it's not really about how big and vast your "magic kingdom" is as much as what you've built—whether or not you've followed God's design for it, and whether or not you use it to serve and bless others and bring glory to God.

Walt Disney's magic kingdom continues to bring smiles to millions of families around the world.

This world and the next can be changed by the legacy of your kingdom.

The principles are proven. The opportunity is real. The invitation is extended.

The only question is: What are you going to build with the opportunities for leadership that God has placed in your hands?

As Walt Disney realized while sitting on a bench in Griffith Park, the greatest adventures begin with an unwavering vision and having enough faith to take the first steps toward making it as real as what is right in front of your face.

Welcome to your magic kingdom of leadership.

Are you ready to build it?

The adventure begins now.

Suggested Reading

For Spiritual Leadership –

The Bible (pick your favorite translation)

For More Inspiration from Walt Disney –

How to Be Like Walt – Pat Williams
Walt Disney: An American Original – Bob Thomas
Lead Like Walt – Pat Williams
The Gospel According to Disney – Phillip Anderson
The Quotable Walt Disney – Dave Smith
The Magic Kingdom – Steven Watts
Walt Disney's America – Christopher Finch
The Disney Touch – Ron Grover

and probably 1,000+ others

About the Author

D r. **William B. Brunson** (Bill) has served in pastoral ministry for over thirty-five years. He currently serves as Senior Pastor of Vestavia Hills Methodist Church in Vestavia Hills, Alabama, where he leads a vibrant congregation of approximately 3,400 members.

A Maxwell Leadership Certified coach and speaker, and a Certified DISC Consultant, Bill brings a unique perspective that integrates biblical wisdom with proven leadership principles. He has a particular gift for helping people discover their purpose and potential, connecting the dots between faith and the leadership challenges they face every day.

Bill is also the author of *There is More: Moving Beyond Cultural Christianity to a Life of Purpose, Passion, and Power*, and *Help and Hope: Devotionals by a Caregiver for Caregivers*. His writing reflects his core conviction that God uses everything—even unexpected sources—to teach us how to lead and live with greater impact.

When he's not preaching, writing, or leading, Bill enjoys spending time with his wife Michelle, their children, and their grandchildren.

Connect with Bill

For speaking opportunities, bulk book orders, coaching inquiries, or to learn about Bill's ministry—he can be reached through vhmc.org, deeperpurposecoaching.com, or by email: bill@deeperpurposecoaching.com